LEGENDARY L

[signatures] Julie D Wa...

LEGENDARY LANDSCAPES

SECRETS OF ANCIENT WILTSHIRE REVEALED

J.D. WAKEFIELD

NOD PRESS

Published by
Nod Press PO Box 338
Marlborough
Wiltshire SN8 4PW

ISBN 0 9536301 0 2

Cover artwork by Bridget Stevens

Typeset, printed and bound in Great Britain by
Avonset, Bath

This book is dedicated to our Grandparents

ACKNOWLEDGEMENTS

We are indebted to Kevin Redpath for his invaluable help and advice. We are also grateful to John Michell for his comments on the manuscript when it was in its infancy; and to Nick Riley for bringing the photograph of the Silbury Hag to our attention. A very special thank-you to Bridget Stevens and Nick Riley for the beautiful artwork they have contributed to the book, for their encouragement and their support. Finally, we would like to express our gratitude to the Carson family, especially Polly Carson.

PHOTOGRAPHIC ACKNOWLEDGEMENTS

Permission to reproduce plates has kindly been given by the following who retain the copyright:
Crown copyright material is reproduced by permission of English Heritage acting under licence from the Controller of Her Majesty's Stationery Office. The photograph on page 58 is reproduced courtesy of Wiltshire County Council, Education and Libraries. Permission to reproduce the photograph on page 83 was given by the Alexander Keiller Museum, Avebury.

Every effort has been made to trace all present copyright holders of the material used in this book. Any omission is unintentional and we will be pleased to correct any errors in future editions.

CONTENTS

List of Illustrations ix

Introduction 1

1   A Monumental Legacy 3

2   Peering through the Veil 11

3   Adam, Eve and Serpent 19

4   All the World's a Stage 37

5   The Hag of Silbury Hill 55

6   The Mysteries of Avebury 79

7   Cradle of a Nation 95

Notes 106

Select Bibliography 114

Index 118

LIST OF ILLUSTRATIONS

Photography by John David Wakefield unless otherwise stated.
Illustrations by Bridget Stevens and Nick Riley.

	page
Photo of Silbury Hill	3
Block diagram of Silbury Hill	5
The Silbury Mother Goddess (after Michael Dames)	6
Goddess figurine from Turkey	6
Map showing Avebury and part of the Vale of Pewsey	7
Photo of the Alton Barnes White Horse	8
The Alton Goddess. Drawing by Nick Riley	10
Goddess of Willendorf	12
Goddess of Lespugue	12
Goddess of Laussel	13
Goddess from Grimes Graves, Norfolk	14
The Gumelniţa embracing couple (after Marija Gimbutas)	15
Cairn on the Paps of Anu, Ireland. Photo: Nick Riley	18
Photo of Adam's Grave long barrow	20
Photo of West Kennet long barrow	21
Ground plan of West Kennet long barrow	21
Photo of the barrow and serpentine bank on Knap Hill	25
Close-up of serpentine bank	26
Serpent Goddess	27
Serpent Goddess with baby snake (after Marija Gimbutas)	27
Minoan Priestess with snakes and ceremonial apron	27
The Lady of Pazardzik	28
Goddess from Tel Azmak, Bulgaria	28
Photo of triangular sarsen stone	30
Masonic apron. Drawing by Nick Riley	30
Photo of Knap Hill causewayed enclosure	31
Photo of carving in All Saints Church, All Cannings	32
Carving in Avebury Church	33
William Stukeley's Serpent Temple.	34
Photo of the Adam and Eve stones, Avebury	35
Knap Hill triangular enclosure	38
Figurine with columnar neck	39
Goddess of Hamangia	39
Photo highlighting the extended 'neck' of the Alton Goddess	40
Photo of the serpentine bank leading into East Field	41

Artistic impression of the Alton Goddess by Bridget Stevens 41
The dancing shaman at Les Trois Frères 45
Photo of Alton Priors springs 48
Photo of the Sutton Benger Green Man 52
The 'Corn Jack Mummers' on Silbury Hill
    Photo: Julie Dawn Wakefield 53
Hag figure from Notgrove, Gloucestershire 55
Flint 'hag' found in West Kennet long barrow 55
Aerial view of Silbury Hill (highlighting the 'Silbury Hag')
    Photo: © Crown copyright. NMR 56
Close-up of the 'Silbury Hag'. Photo: © Crown copyright. NMR 56
Aerial view of the 'Silbury Hag'. Photo: courtesy of Wiltshire
    County Council, Education and Libraries. 58
Artistic impression of 'The Silbury Trinity' by Nick Riley 59
Female figure on an Etruscan bronze plate 70
Sheela-na-gig at Bully, Calvados 70
Viking slab at Gotland, Sweden 71
Sheela-na-gig on an Irish round tower 71
Oak figurine from Ballachulish, Scotland 72
Sheela-na-gig at Oaksey, Wiltshire 72
Photo of Sheela-na-gig at Winterbourne Monkton Church,
    Wiltshire. 74
The god Pan at Silbury Hill. Drawing by Bridget Stevens 76
Full moon axis alignment (after Michael Dames) 80
Carvings on the West Kennet Avenue
    Photo: courtesy of the Alexander Keiller Museum, Avebury. 83
The Ouroboros carving at Avebury. Drawing by Nick Riley 84
Silbury Hill with serpentine path. Drawing by William Stukeley 86
The Omphalos of Delphi (after Buffie Johnson) 87
Photo of the Runic Nod carved on stone 8, Avebury. 88
Close-up of Runic Nod carving 89
Tau Cross and the Runic Nod. Drawing by J.D. Wakefield 92
The Great Pyramid, Egypt. Drawing by Nick Riley. 93
The Great Pyramid and the solar flare
    Drawing by Nick Riley 94
Photo of the Devil's Chair, Avebury 98
Close-up of 'the face' in the Devil's Chair. 98
Sketch of 'the face' in the Devil's Chair by Nick Riley 98
Aerial view of 'The Silbury Hag'
    Photo: © Crown copyright. NMR 105

INTRODUCTION

A visit in July 1996 to a redundant church in the village of Alton Priors, Wiltshire, provided the inspiration for this book. All Saints Church is situated in the meadow of Alton Priors, which lies in the heart of the Vale of Pewsey. The surrounding hills are adorned with prehistoric monuments and, in the words of the Wiltshire poet Richard Jefferies, they are 'alive with the dead'. Standing in the churchyard is a 2000 year old female yew tree whose hollow centre offers a secluded bower. Around the tree are several graves, and an old churchyard tale concerning yew trees in general is that their roots extend into the mouths of the buried dead, retrieve their untold secrets and transform them 'into whispers to be blown loose from the foliage in the wind.'[1]

On that sunny July day the tree provided the ideal shady spot to rest and contemplate religion, particularly the spiritual beliefs of the Neolithic (New Stone Age) peoples. What motivated them to build their stone and earthen churches that now lie redundant like the church of All Saints? Whilst sitting in the tree the doors of perception opened, and an untold secret floated on the breeze into the gnarled hermitage. The landscape whispered that the first clue to unravelling the entangled strands of prehistory is to access the myths prevalent in that era. This can be achieved, despite having no written record of life during the New Stone Age. Archæology provides a firm basis with which to start, along with relevant folklore and traditions upheld by rural communities, but the key element to decoding ancient monuments is to recognize their relevance within the surrounding landscape.

Lucien Lévy-Bruhl found that the Marind people of Papua New Guinea cannot view their environment without feeling the presence of the mythic ancestors. For them the surrounding countryside is a living book 'in which the myths are inscribed ... a legend is captured in the very outlines of the landscape'.[2] The Aborigines believe that Australia is covered with Songlines that record the legends of the creation of the land. At various sacred spots known as 'story places' the mythic ancestors created plants and animals during the 'Dreamtime', and established rituals for their descendants to uphold. Aborigines still walk the lines today, singing the sacred songs and re-enacting the ancient customs to strengthen the power of the Songlines. In this way, the people connect with the land, and the latent deities and Spirits are re-awakened.

The legends, ancestral lineage, rites and ancient mysteries of Pagan Celtic Britain and Ireland were preserved in poetry, song and prose by the Bards of the Druid caste. This body of sacred knowledge was maintained by an oral tradition, and Bards were required to undergo many years of training. The Bards memorized the mythic history of the burial mounds, recited the stories associated with rocks and standing stones, and were taught the tales of all the trees along with their alphabetical relevance. Our Neolithic forebears possessed this mythopoeic perception, and felt compelled to set their poems and stories in stone and earth in the landscapes that inspired them.

This book is an invitation to retrace the Songlines that stretch across the Vale of Pewsey and the vast sacred precinct of Avebury: two of the most important ritual landscapes of ancient Wiltshire yet they have often been overshadowed by Stonehenge. Making this journey will hopefully lead to a greater understanding of prehistoric cultures, and shed light on many of the unsolved mysteries of Wiltshire.

J.D. Wakefield
Wiltshire, 1999

CHAPTER ONE

A MONUMENTAL LEGACY

The true mystery of the world is the visible not the invisible
(Oscar Wilde)

The county of Wiltshire, part of the ancient English region of Wessex, was described by Thomas Hardy as having 'a partly real, partly dream' quality. It is a land of mystery and magic that offers a window on the past with its profusion of prehistoric monuments, particularly in the Avebury area. Silbury Hill, the tallest artificial mound in Europe, and the impressive remains of Avebury's stone circles, stone avenues and colossal henge are just several of the many rich sites that comprise the Avebury complex. The neighbouring downs are littered with clusters of various barrows, including West Kennet long barrow, the largest in England and Wales. Avebury was undoubtedly one of the most important places in ancient Britain, and today it attracts tens of thousands of visitors from across the world each year, eager to witness and to comprehend the legacy that was left by prehistoric peoples. Why were these monuments built; what secrets do they hold?

These questions were asked regarding Silbury Hill for example.

Silbury Hill surrounded by the winter floods.

Silbury stands 130 feet (40 m) high and 520 feet (159 m) in diameter in the valley floor of the River Kennet, and is one mile to the south of Avebury. It is surrounded by a ditch which contains two causeways of untouched chalk and the whole monument occupies 5½ acres (2 ha) of land. The writer John Aubrey recorded in the seventeenth century that 'No history gives any account of this hill. The tradition only is that King Sil, or Zel, as the country folke pronounce, was buried here on horseback, and that the hill was raysed while a posset of milke was seething.'[1] According to local tradition the King rides around the hill on moonlit nights wearing golden armour.[2]

Aubrey, William Stukeley and several other antiquarians concluded that Silbury Hill was the gigantic grave of a mighty monarch who had been buried with his horse and royal treasure. In 1776, Colonel Drax and tin miners from Cornwall were employed by the Duke of Northumberland to dig vertically from the centre of Silbury in an attempt to discover King Sil. He could not be found, however, and the treasure amounted to a mere slip of oak wood. During the Victorian era King Sil transmogriphied into a golden statue: 'There is at this day a local tradition that a horse and rider, the size of life and of solid gold, yet remains below.'[3] Excavations led by J. Merewether were carried out at Silbury in 1849. He noted in his diary that the digs were frowned upon by the superstitious locals, and a gothic thunderstorm that occurred whilst the men were tunnelling into the hill was perceived as divine confirmation of the villagers' beliefs:

The weather on this day was very unfavourable; and at night – much to the satisfaction, I have no doubt, of the rustics, whose notions respecting the examination of Silbury and the opening of the barrows were not divested of superstitious dread, – one of the most grand and tremendous thunder-storms I ever recollect to have witnessed, made the hills re-echo to the crashing peals, and Silbury itself, as the men asserted who were working in its centre, to tremble to its base, – although they could not see the flashes of violet-coloured lightning which lit up the broad expanse of hills, and defined their outline in their most distant range.[4]

The booty retrieved from the Merewether dig consisted of deer antlers and fragments of mistletoe.

Flinders Petrie excavated Silbury in 1922, and in 1959 Dr McKim conducted a resistivity survey; like previous excavators they searched in vain for the burial chamber that housed King Sil. In 1967, Professor Richard Atkinson and a team of specialists tunnelled into Silbury and carried out detailed examinations of the hill and immediate surroundings. The team believed that Silbury was a Bronze Age barrow that contained an important burial. To the disappointment of the project they discovered there was no interment at Silbury, no elaborate grave goods – just a few votive offerings such as antlers and twisted pieces of grass. The excavations did

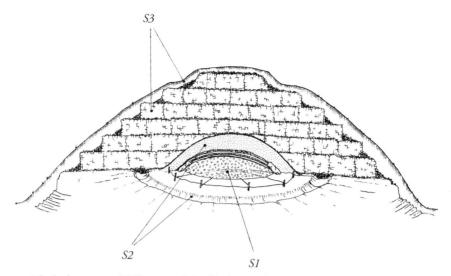

Block diagram of Silbury Hill highlighting the complexity that went into the construction. S1 primary mound; S2 chalk mound and ditch; S3 6 tiers composed of radial concentric chalk walls infilled with rubble, and the entire mound covered with turf.

reveal, however, the astounding complexity of the internal structure of Silbury, and that there was deliberation in the design.

Silbury was built in three phases, commencing around 2700 BC with the construction of Silbury 1, the primary mound. A wattle fence 65.6 feet (20 m) in diameter was initially built onto the original land surface that was supported by widely spaced stakes to form a broad circle. A small mound of clay with flints 16 feet (5 m) in diameter and 3 feet (0.8 m) high was built in the centre of the circular enclosed area, and from this mound radiated lengths of twisted grass string. The land surface inside the fence was subsequently covered by a pile of stacked turf and soil. The previous deposits and the fence were then enclosed by four consecutive layers of soil, chalk, clay and river gravel. Several reclining sarsen stones were discovered at the sides of the circular mound, upon which were fragments of animal bone, antlers and mistletoe. A second mound (Silbury 2) was placed over the initial mound using chalk rubble hewn from an encircling ditch, but this ditch was then refilled and a much larger ditch was dug. Blocks of chalk were used from the new ditch to create stepped walls that were infilled with chalk rubble (Silbury 3). Six tiers were raised and the entire intricate stepped-cone structure was then covered with soil and turf. The complex layering that was employed in Silbury's construction led Professor Atkinson to conclude that the designers of the hill were 'obsessively concerned with stability'. Silbury is a unique and unprecedented feat of engineering and as a testimony to that achievement it has retained its original shape.

The results of the 1967 excavation showed that Silbury was over 4,500 years old, therefore it was built during the Neolithic period (the New Stone Age), and not the Bronze Age as had previously been supposed. The archæologists also found that the original turf displayed green grass and that the grass had preserved the remains of winged ants and other insects. From this they were able to ascertain that the turf had been cut and stacked in early August because ants would not have developed wings prior to that period. It has been estimated that it took 18 million hours of labour to complete Silbury,[5] and considering that the work was carried out with the most rudimentary tools – antler picks, woven wicker baskets and the shoulder blades of oxen for shovels – it was an incredible undertaking. Silbury was obviously not sepulchral in purpose so what was it, and why had such tremendous effort been expended on its construction?

The author Michael Dames was the first to un-earth the true meaning behind Silbury. In his pioneering work *The Silbury Treasure: The Great Goddess Rediscovered* Dames highlighted that the hill was a physical representation of a pregnant mother goddess – a massive piece of Neolithic art and ingenuity. Not only was the mound itself her huge womb, but the structure in its entirety with the ditch and causeways was designed to retain water from the underground springs, and all these features plus surrounding water-filled moat defined the body of a pregnant squatting woman about to give birth.[6]

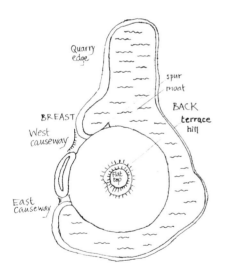

The Silbury Mother Goddess.

Painted pot goddess from Hacilar, Turkey, that displays a similarity to the Silbury Goddess.

Silbury was the complete antithesis of the myth that scholars had perpetuated; it was not built to honour the death of a great patriarch – but to celebrate the life-giving forces of the Mother Goddess.

Was Silbury the only Mother Goddess sculpted in the Neolithic era in Wiltshire, or could others still remain that have not been previously recognized?

Our investigation begins in the Vale of Pewsey, part of the Marlborough downland in North Wiltshire, just three miles as the crow flies from Silbury Hill. The area is one of outstanding beauty, with its stretches of farmland and spectacular, undulating hills. Nestling in the heart of the Vale are the quaint, sleepy villages of All Cannings, Stanton-St-Bernard, Alton Barnes and Alton Priors. The range of hills that are relevant to this study are those of the south-facing escarpment, described by H.J. Massingham as being one of 'the purest landscapes'.[7]

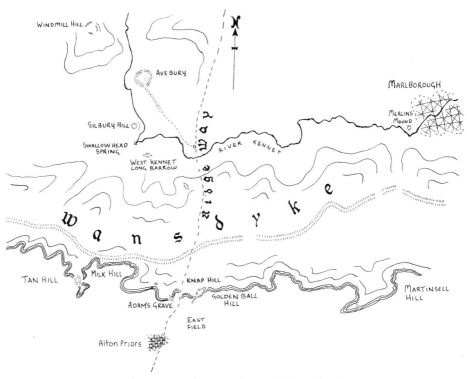

Map showing Avebury and part of the Vale of Pewsey.

Beginning with Tan Hill, this along with Milk Hill are the highest points in Wiltshire at just over 900 feet (294 m). Up until 1932 a fair was held annually in August on Tan Hill's summit, which was the highlight of the farming year in the Pewsey Vale. There is a legend that the body of Queen Guinevere and her funeral cortege travelled over this hill at night, on their way to her interment at Glastonbury where her husband King Arthur was buried.[8] On the pinnacle of Milk Hill is a barrow, and a white horse was carved into the side of the hill in 1812. John Green, an old man from All Cannings, told author Kathleen Wiltshire in 1940 that at midnight the white horse would come down off Milk Hill to drink from the dewpond near Cannings Cross, and other villagers affirmed that they had often seen the horse at the top end of All Cannings.[9]

The adjacent Walker's Hill is capped by a Neolithic chambered barrow known as Adam's Grave: 'the most dramatically sited long barrow in Wiltshire and possibly in Wessex.'[10] According to local folklore a giant emerges from Adam's Grave if a person runs around it seven times.[11] The prehistoric trackway known as the Ridgeway crosses the col between Walker's Hill and Knap Hill, along which sarsen stones were brought from the Marlborough Downs to build Stonehenge.

The Alton Barnes White Horse.

Knap Hill is surmounted by a Neolithic causewayed camp established around 3500 BC. A causewayed camp is an oval or circular enclosure built by the early farmers, usually on a hilltop, and surrounded by concentric banks and ditches. The ditches being interrupted by numerous causeways of untouched chalk. Their purpose is somewhat confusing for there is no evidence that they were permanent settlements, and they do not seem to have been used as fortresses. The term 'causewayed camp' is therefore deceiving and some writers prefer to call them causewayed enclosures. The enclosure on Knap Hill is reputed to contain treasure[12] and it overlooks the expansive East Field. It shows no evidence of defence and Sir R.C. Hoare stated that he could 'discover no apparent signs of any extensive British population'[13] at the enclosure on Knap Hill. Furthermore, an unusual serpentine bank and ditch that leaves the enclosure and runs down the most precipitous part of Knap Hill has no logical function. Knap Hill is connected to Golden Ball Hill in the east by a level saddle of triangular shaped land, onto which a triangular enclosure was built in the Late Celtic era. Archæologists recently uncovered what appears to be the remains of a Mesolithic camp on Golden Ball Hill, which indicates that it was inhabited 7000 years ago and is perhaps, the oldest communal dwelling in Britain.[14]

The seemingly unconnected prehistoric sites built onto the hills around Alton pose several puzzling questions for archæologists. Ancient harmonies resonate across the landscape but they are frustratingly inaudible. The legends of sleeping giants, Queen Guinevere and hidden treasure hint that there is something to be discovered in this area of the Pewsey Vale, something to be learnt about the personality of the place. When the hills are viewed from the east the secret is revealed, for the hills and the Neolithic sites built onto them create the impression of a recumbent woman who has just given birth. The natural jutting spur from Walker's Hill is an elongated neck. Milk Hill and Walker's Hill form two huge breasts, and the barrows that crown them create a nipple effect. Knap Hill is a pregnant belly, the unusual bank running down it is the umbilical cord, and a low bowl-shaped barrow alongside the bank is a swollen navel. Guinevere is here! This gigantic 'woman' part natural, part artificially made seems to depict a goddess figure who has just given birth into the field below her – the East Field.

The Neolithic people appear to have placed particular sites onto the natural rolling hills to accentuate their womanly shape; so much so that they have created an incredible architectural icon. Could this really be possible – or could the position of the monuments that seem to make up this female form be mere coincidence, and not intentional at all? Let us part the mists that conceal the remote past to discover who this Goddess was, and then we can begin to determine the role she played in the Pewsey Vale.

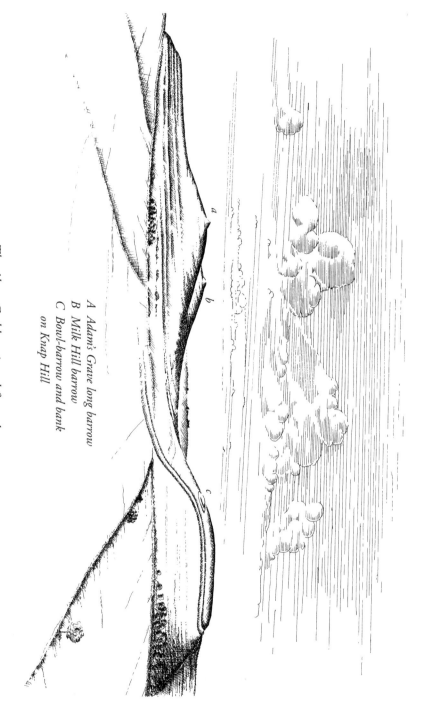

a
b
c

A Adam's Grave long barrow
B Milk Hill barrow
C Bowl-barrow and bank
   on Knap Hill

The Alton Goddess viewed from the east.

CHAPTER TWO

PEERING THROUGH THE VEIL

I am the queen: of every hive

From The Song of Amergin
(An ancient Celtic calendar poem,
trans. Robert Graves.)[1]

The oldest art objects in the world are the crudely sculpted images of female figures and animals that have been found in various countries, dating to a period of prehistory known as the Lower Palæolithic, around 500,000 years ago. The people that lived during this era were hunter-gatherers that followed the migratory herds, and inhabited caves and rock shelters. Several caves, such as those of northern Spain and south-west France, have revealed breathtaking Palæolithic artistic imagery – animal scenes; female fertility symbols and male semi-human figures. Several of the paintings are in areas that are relatively inaccessible or in deep recesses; others have subsequent paintings superimposed on them repeatedly, whilst adjacent walls are completely bare. This suggests, as Fernand Windels says, 'a deliberate pursuit of the mysterious and secret; in fact, a ritual intention.'[2] The caves do appear to have been sanctuaries for initiation rituals and ceremonies related to life, death and rebirth – the caves themselves being envisaged as wombs. This is echoed in language for in Sumerian '*matu* meant "womb", "underworld", and "sacred cave" from the universal root for "mother" – hence Latin and pre-Teutonic *mater*, and Old Teutonic *modar*.'[3] There are many examples of vulvas engraved on rock surfaces in caves, some of which are reddened with ochre which was symbolic of life-giving blood. The carvings date by tool association to around 30,000 BC. Natural fissures and niches within the caves have also been found painted with red ochre which suggests that they were perceived as the ubiquitous vulva.

The parietal and mobiliary art of this epoch conveys sophisticated, symbolic messages which in turn provides an insight into the religious beliefs prevalent during the Palæolithic. There is a paucity of art of this kind in Britain because the last Ice Age rendered many areas uninhabitable from approximately 23,000 – 12,000 BC.[4] This was a significant period of artistic expression in other parts of Europe and when Britain became more hospitable the migrating hunters brought these religious concepts with them. There are innumerable figurines dating from the Upper Palæolithic, around 40,000 – 10,000 years ago. The miniature sculptures are almost exclusively female, with pendulous breasts, exaggerated buttocks and pregnant bellies. The statuettes are icons, representations of a primordial deity – the life-giving Goddess.

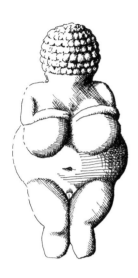

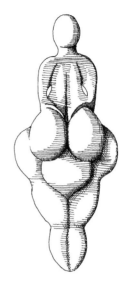

The Goddess of Willendorf, Austria, 30,000 BC.

The Goddess of Lespugue, 23,000 BC.

The Goddess was Nature personified; the embodiment of fecundity; the source of all creation, and the recipient of the dead. Palæolithic peoples often buried their dead in the foetal position or sprinkled them with red ochre, which demonstrates that they believed the dead would return to the Goddess, to then be reborn. A male skeleton stained with red ochre that was discovered in the Paviland Cave in Wales is one such example.

The moon was a visible symbol of the Goddess changing from horned crescent moon, to pregnant full moon, to the dark moon. It contained the mysteries of the universe – of birth (crescent), life (full), death (dark), and rebirth (crescent). Women were connected to the moon due to the monthly menstrual cycle and were the living reminder of its phases as Maiden (young crescent moon), Mother (full pregnant moon), and Hag (waning and dark moon). The moon also provided early cultures with a way of measuring time:

'The importance of the moon as a first clock is enshrined in language; in which the name for moon also provides the words measurement, month and menstruation. The English word month is connected with the moon; in Latin *mensis* means month and *mensura* is measurement, which also gives us the lunar-based menstrual cycle.'[5]

A representation of the Goddess was carved on the outer wall at the entrance to a Palæolithic rock shelter at Laussel in the Dordogne. Her left hand points to her vulva and in her raised right hand she holds a bison horn that has thirteen notches, corresponding to the thirteen months of the old lunar calendar – the horn itself symbolizing the crescent moon. There are traces of red ochre on her body.

The Goddess of Laussel, France, holds a bison horn with thirteen notches that correspond to the thirteen months of the old lunar calendar. Her other hand points to her vulva indicating the synchronization between the female menstrual cycle and the lunar cycle; the notched horn heralds the birth of the science of measuring time.
(c. *20,000 BC*)

The Goddess occasionally appeared alongside an animal manifestation of a male consort. The image of a pregnant goddess who is lying under the legs and penis of a bison was found carved onto a piece of reindeer bone at Laugerie Basse in the Dordogne. The bison symbolized virility and so this bone, approximately 15,000 years old, could be a depiction of the myth of the Sacred Marriage – the union of the deities.

The Goddess religion was upheld for tens of thousands of years, continuing through the Mesolithic (Middle Stone Age) and into the Neolithic (*c.* 4500 BC – 2500 BC). The Neolithic period saw the arrival of people from the Mediterranean and Eastern Europe into Britain and Ireland who possessed the knowledge of agriculture. They cleared woodland; introduced cereals such as emmer wheat, barley and flax, and established grassland on which to graze domesticated cattle, pigs and sheep. They also produced pottery and settled in farming communities which created a more predictable food supply, and a more permanent lifestyle than the nomadic life of earlier peoples. The focus naturally shifted from the sanctity of the cave to the sacrality of the local landscape that was perceived as a living deity – the Goddess. In various regions flint was mined, and in south-west Norfolk at Grimes Graves, the chalk figure of a pregnant goddess was discovered at the bottom of a spent flint mine shaft.

Goddess found in the Neolithic flint mines at Grimes Graves, Norfolk, 2850 BC.

Alongside the figurine were a carved chalk phallus, chalk balls, seven red deer antlers and a chalk cup that had been placed in the base of a pile of flint shaped into a triangle. These are clearly ritual objects, propitiatory offerings to the Goddess in the hope that she would provide more flint.

The identity of the Goddess was redefined in this agricultural era because in addition to aiding in fertility, pregnancy and parturition she was also relied upon to prevent crop failure and droughts, and to nourish and protect livestock. The Goddess was envisaged as a three-in-one Trinity who was equated with the cycle of the seasons. In springtime she was the Maiden, in summer she was the Mother who gave birth to the crops, and when the ground was frozen and trees were bare she was the Winter Hag. The assistance of each aspect was invoked through rituals that were performed at specific times in the seasonal calendar, a crucial event being the harvest. The harvest ceremonies and celebrations took place in early August, the time that construction first began on Silbury Hill. This was a key festival in the Neolithic agrarian year, and continued to be so during Celtic times when it was known as *Lughnasadh*.

Images of a human male god began to appear in the Neolithic period along with a developed version of the theme of the *hieros gamos* – the Sacred Marriage of the Goddess and the God. The union of the male and female principles assured the continuation of the cycles, the Goddess then giving birth to the Sacred Child – the harvest. Marija Gimbutas explains that the concept of the Divine Child 'was at the heart of the whole complex of images of an agrarian religion, and represents the most traditional of motifs.'[6] A possible depiction of the Divine Marriage dating from the fifth millennium BC was recovered from the Balkans.

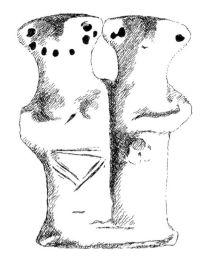

The Gumelniţa embracing couple, late fifth millennium BC. The female is not depicted as a pregnant goddess, she is a maiden, and the couple appear to be a portrayal of the concept of the Divine Marriage.

The most significant aspect of the New Stone Age was the introduction of massive communal constructions. The first monuments to be built were causewayed enclosures and long barrows; followed by wooden circles, henges, linear cursuses, stone circles, stone avenues and isolated standing stones. The moon displayed the three aspects of the Goddess, the sun was often seen as male, and so many of the monuments were aligned to these celestial bodies to incorporate the myth of the Divine Marriage. The relationship of the sites to the land was also important; the monuments and the natural topography together formed 'the architectural whole.'[7] The Silbury Mother Goddess was strategically placed in the valley floor of the Kennet because of the sacred significance of the river, and its source the Swallowhead spring. Ancient races perceived rivers and springs as being intensely numinous; they were the life-giving waters that flowed directly from the Goddess. The Neolithic farmers chose to construct Silbury Hill – a large image of the Mother Goddess – to blend harmoniously with her holy waters.

In the Vale of Pewsey, prehistoric people had perceived the contours of the landscape as the body of the Mother Goddess. There are countless hills and mountain ranges across the world that have been seen as recumbent forms of the Goddess. A mountain near San Francisco is called *Tamalpais* by the Native Americans, which means 'the Maiden'.[8] The Pairc hills near Callanish stone circle on the Scottish Isle of Lewis, naturally form the profile of a sleeping woman. The locals still call the hills 'the Sleeping Beauty'. At the major southern standstill of the moon (every 18.6 years), the full moon is seen to rise out of the Sleeping Beauty's body and travel up to her head; as the moon begins to set it then appears to fall into the centre of the stone circle. This is sheer poetry: a mystical fusion of the moon, landscape

Goddess and the Neolithic stone circle. Vincent Scully noticed that temple sites in ancient Greece were built where the presence of a deity 'had been previously recognized in the natural topography. The temple served to amplify and render more accessible the sacred qualities of the *genius loci.*'[9] What makes the Goddess figure in the Pewsey Vale so remarkable is that prehistoric monuments were actually built onto the hills to represent various parts of her body, which then enhanced her female form already personified in the land.

At some stage in the New Stone Age the Goddess in Britain seems to have acquired the name Ane, Ann or Ana. Ane was 'the great Earth Mother, from which the Welsh royal families traced their line … the pre-Celtic Ane, mother of the gods.'[10] Many authors agree that the British goddess Ann is pre-Celtic and her name is therefore associated with the late Neolithic. In his book *Secret Shrines*, Paul Broadhurst describes a carving in stone of the face of a mother goddess at a holy well in Whitstone, Cornwall: 'the link with prehistory is tangible as the ancient face peers out at us, from the time, perhaps of the Neolithic religion of the great Goddess Ana.'[11] The name Ane/Ana seems to have been used for the Goddess worldwide in various forms. In Britain she was Ann, Ane, Ana and Annis. In Ireland she was Anu, Anann and Aine. In Sumeria she was In-Anna or Anna-Nin. The Babylonians called her Anahita and the ancient Armenians adopted this name for their goddess of wisdom and fertility. In Syria she was Anat or Anatha and in Phoenicia Anthyt. Further goddesses were fashioned from the root An/Ana – the Greek goddesses Diana and Athena were Di-*ana* and Ath-e*ana*, and the Celtic Arianrhod and Cretan Ariadne were Ar-i*an*-rhod and Ar-i-*an*-de.[12] Robert Graves writes: 'if one needs a single, simple, inclusive name for the Great Goddess, Ana is the best choice. To Christian mystics she is "God's Grandmother".'[13]

The Celts naturally included Ann in their religion, and introduced a maiden goddess known as Bride, Brigid, Brid or Bridget. Ann and Bride were responsible for the fertility of the land and waters and numerous sites were dedicated to these two goddesses. The cult surrounding them was so strong that the Christian Church had no choice but to absorb these eponymous goddesses into Christianity in the guise of Saint Anne and Saint Bride/Brigid. St Anne was the patron saint of childbirth and the alleged mother of the Virgin Mary, however, in the Bible Mary's parents are not named; the pagan Mother Goddess Ann was clearly conflated with the saint. Places associated with Ann and Bride were re-dedicated to St Anne and St Bride, for as Aubrey Burl explains: 'The Christian Church did not weed out paganism. It came to terms with it and the two grew together, intertwined, so that some of our most ancient past is still with us.' Could any fragments of prehistory have survived through the succession of the Church that could confirm the existence of the Alton Goddess as a mythologised figure?

Placenames provide the clues to ancient religious practices and the presence of local deities, and Tan Hill is an outstanding example for it was previously called 'St

Anne's Hill'. On Saxton's map of 1611 it is simply known as 'Ann's Hill'. A fair took place on top of the hill that was recorded in a Charter Roll of 1499 as 'the feast and morrow of St Anne'.[14] Known as St Anne's Fair it occurred on August 6th–7th and continued to be held on the hill until 1932. Tan Hill is one of the highest points in Wiltshire, and it is several miles from the nearest village. T. Story-Maskelyne remarked that 'it must strike all who have visited this spot that this is a remarkable place to have been chosen for a fair. A fair is generally held at a place rendered easily accessible by means of good roads or water ways.'[15] This is not the case at Tan Hill/Ann's Hill and so it is unusual that such an isolated spot should have been selected for a fair: 'Such a place could never have been originally chosen merely for this purpose.'[16] J. Thurnam wrote: 'There can be little doubt that this hill has been the site of pagan rites'.[17]

In France, barefoot pilgrims would climb the hills on Saint Anne's day.[18] Fairs were held at St Anne d'Auray, Brittany on August 6th; at St Anne de Palue in early August. Baring Gould describes a place in Brittany called Keranna, meaning 'the caer or camp of Anna.' He identifies Anna 'with a goddess of the Celts, or of even older Dolmen builders whom they had subjugated. It is now the site of the pilgrim's church of St Anne d'Auray.'[19] Gould informs us that, 'in 1623 a peasant, Yves Nicolazie, dug up a statue on the spot … he supposed it to be St Anne. The Carmelites heard of it and organised a cult of the image in 1627, and St Anne is now regarded as the special patroness of Brittany, as Anna seems to have been of old, showing how old beliefs hang on, and reassert themselves in changed forms.'[20] This is undoubtedly the case at Tan Hill for its former name was Ann's Hill.

The Celtic harvest festival of Lughnasadh that occurred in early August on Tan Hill was replaced and syncretized to St Anne's Fair. The Celtic festival itself was a continuation of the Neolithic harvest ceremony that was celebrated at the same time of year, on a hilltop, and was concerned with the supplication of the Goddess, who came to be known as Ann. All Saints Church in the nearby village of All Cannings was previously dedicated to St Anne, and so the name of the hill, the fair and the church are all echoes of the veneration of the pregnant goddess Ann – a physical representation of whom was etched onto these very hills. (It is refreshing to hear that there are plans to re-dedicate the chancel of All Saints to St Anne.)

In the valley between Tan Hill and Rybury is a small stone circle comprised of nine stones. An Anglo-Saxon charter mentions some stones that were used as a boundary marker between All Cannings and Stanton-St-Bernard.[21] Tan Hill is in the parish of All Cannings so the stone circle must be the stones in question. On the charter the stones were named as the 'Anan stones', which again would seem to be a link with the Goddess as Anann, or Anu, was the name of the Mother of the Gods in Ireland. There are twin mountains in Ireland that resemble breasts which are emphasized by the nipple-shaped cairns built onto their summits. The mountains are known in Gaelic as *Dhá Chíoch Anann*, the 'Paps or breasts of Anu'.

Nipple-shaped cairn on the 'Paps of Anu', Ireland.

Tan Hill and surrounding area were connected by name to the Alton Goddess, so what of the hills that delineate her body?

CHAPTER THREE

ADAM, EVE AND SERPENT

I have been a snake enchanted on a hill

From the *Câd Goddeu*
(trans. John Matthews)[1]

The two hills that form the breasts of the Alton Goddess are Milk Hill and Walker's Hill. Milk Hill must surely have been so named to intimate its breast-like appearance. In 1425 the hill was noted as Melkenhylle[2], and the Saxon term *Melk* is an adjective that means 'giving milk'[3] – so it literally means, the milk-giving hill. The Celtic word for milk was 'Melc', so it seems highly likely that Milk Hill has always retained that title. The tumulus on Milk Hill that is now un-named on modern maps was formerly known as Black Barrow, for it appears on a charter as early as 957 AD with that name. On the Andrewes and Dury map of 1773 it is called Black burrow. The Reverend A.C. Smith informs us that Black Barrow derives its name from 'the Anglo-Saxon *blac*, "shining," "white," as if the French *blanc*; and not the modern English word *black*, with the contrary meaning.'[4] It seems more than just coincidence that the hill that is the left breast of the Alton Goddess could have been called Milk Hill for thousands of years, and that the barrow on that hill that forms the nipple was named 'white' barrow – white being the operative adjective to describe the Goddess' milk. This barrow was excavated in the late 1800s and was found to contain no interment or grave goods, so it cannot be considered as a Bronze Age round barrow. The excavation did damage the original shape of the nipple somewhat – this is clearly visible from the west as the barrow has a sunken crown. It was also the site for the Alton bonfire to commemorate the marriage of the Prince of Wales in the 1800s. The fire on the barrow's summit, and the excavation, means that the nipple is no longer in prime condition. Marked on the Saxton map is a hawthorn bush on Milk Hill that is called 'Ann's Thorn' – this must have been a boundary marker of some kind, and is a name that appears to be connected to Ann the Alton Goddess.

Adam's Grave chambered long barrow is 200 feet (61 m) long and 20 feet (6 m) high, and forms the dramatic image of the prominent right nipple of the Alton Goddess. It is positioned on Walker's Hill which was supposedly named after a former owner, Clement Walker, who died in 1801, but as A.C. Smith states this is not the true derivation:

Adam's Grave Neolithic long barrow, the most prominent feature in the Pewsey Vale landscape.

… Walker's Hill derives its name from the old British trackway, which crosses the hill hard by, and which is described in a charter relating to Alton as *Weala-wege*. The peasants still call the hill "Walc-Way Hill"; and Andrewes and Dury, in their map, though they call it "Walker's Hill", have given underneath the word "Walk-way". This is a very interesting derivation, and there is no doubt that it is the correct one, and that as *Weala-wege*, or the "Welsh way", was the ordinary name for a British road, this is the *weala-wege hill*, or the *Welsh Way*, or *British trackway hill*.[5]

Walker's Hill was the Walkway Hill named after the prehistoric track that crosses it – the Ridgeway. This upland track appears to have been in use for over four thousand years and it is thought to be one of the oldest pathways in Britain. The Ridgeway runs from Buckinghamshire to Wiltshire and joins the Icknield Way that stretches from Hertfordshire. It was a pilgrim route connecting various sacred landscapes and after crossing the Alton Goddess it continues off the Downs and peters out in the field adjacent to Alton Priors church.

The majority of earthen long barrows and megalithic graves of Neolithic Europe are examples of architectural symbolism for they are shaped to imitate the body of the Goddess. T. Cyriax was one of the first archæologists to recognize that the earth under which people were buried was 'the Mother of the dead'. He says:

'The object of the tomb builder would have been to make the tomb as much like the body of a Mother as he was able. The same idea seems to have been carried out in the internal arrangements of the passage grave, with the burial chambers and passage perhaps representing uterus and vagina.'[6] The tomb was the primordial womb of the Goddess, a concept that originated in the Palæolithic era when bodies were buried within the womb caves and sprinkled with ochre. Professor Gimbutas found in her comprehensive study of European burial practices, that the regenerative organs of the Goddess formed the basis of Neolithic tomb designs.[7] Chambers are symbolic of the vagina and uterus and the forecourt areas that lead to them are similar to open legs.[8] Several monuments are anthropomorphic and actually 'replicate the ample contours of the Pregnant Goddess figurine.'[9]

West Kennet long barrow opposite Silbury Hill is an impressive 330 feet (100 m) long, the largest long barrow in England and Wales.

West Kennet long barrow opposite Silbury Hill.

Construction of the long barrow first began around 3700 BC and, like Adam's Grave, it is trapezoidal in design. At the eastern end of West Kennet long barrow is a crescent-shaped forecourt leading to five geometrically designed stone-built burial chambers that open on to an axial passage. The ground plan of the chambers resembles a pregnant squatting goddess. Adam's Grave long barrow, however, is the very nipple of the Mother Goddess atop a huge breast-shaped hill: an image that dominates the Pewsey Vale. Sir R.C. Hoare wrote:

Plan of the chambers of West Kennet long barrow; shrine to the Goddess and a temple for the living, as well as tomb of the dead.

'If I were to fix on any one artificial mound within our county likely to have been appropriated to services of worship, I should name the Long barrow on Walker's Hill, differing from others in its construction, and protected by a bank and ditch towards the north and south.'[10]

The bank and ditch were not constructed for defensive purposes, but to create the nipple effect. The long barrow thus raised ensured that the breast of the Alton Goddess was an unmistakeable feature in the landscape.

Adam's Grave was excavated by J. Thurnam in 1860, who discovered the remains of 3 possibly 4 skeletons within the ruined burial chamber at the east end. Found near the skeletal material was a leaf-shaped flint arrowhead, a similar arrowhead was recovered from West Kennet long barrow. Although arrows had a practical use in the hunting of animals they were also employed in religious rites. In various mythologies across the world they were associated with the moon, the sun, rain and fertility. Arrowheads were believed to have protective powers and in Irish, French, English, Zuñi, and Acoma Indian folklore they were specifically associated with women, children or childbirth.[11] During his excavations Thurnam also found evidence of dry-stone walling in Adam's Grave, and at West Kennet long barrow the spaces between some of the sarsen uprights that formed the walls were filled in with panels of the same walling – oolitic limestone slabs brought from the Bath-Frome region, twenty miles to the west. This limestone was also discovered in the Occupation Area at the West Kennet Avenue in Avebury, and in a pit inside a square enclosure on Windmill Hill, near Avebury, that is believed to have been used for the excarnation of corpses.[12] This indicates that the stone may have had a magico-religious significance connected with the dead.

The disarticulated skeletons of approximately 46 individuals were recovered from the chambers of West Kennet long barrow. Long bones had been stacked against the walls, children's bones had been placed inside crevices between the stones.[13] Many skulls were missing which suggests that they were ritually abstracted from the barrow. Aubrey Burl proposed that the skulls deposited in the ditches on Windmill Hill are most likely the ones that had been removed from the long barrow at West Kennet.[14] The long barrow was obviously a focal point for the local Neolithic community, a place where they came to commune with their ancestors. The six perforated ox bones that were retrieved from the chambers of the barrow could have been small whistles used by the shamans and priestesses to summon the dead.[15] The fragments of around 250 pottery vessels; specifically placed animal bones such as a sharpened boar's tooth and a beaver's tooth, and the offerings of flints and shell beads reveal that it was a place of elaborate ritual – a sanctuary for the living. There is a folktale that at sunrise on the summer solstice a priest and a white hound with red ears can be seen entering West Kennet long barrow.[16] The 'priest' was most likely a Druid, and in Celtic mythology the colour red was used as a metaphor for the Otherworld. There are numerous stories of Bards entering prehistoric burial mounds, or fasting upon them in order to obtain wisdom. This implies that they were used for Bardic initiation and perhaps Neolithic sorcerers used West Kennet long barrow for similar purposes.

Although the majority of long barrows are believed to have been funerary in nature there are several in the Avebury area that were not used for housing the dead. The long barrows at Horslip, South Street, West Woods and Beckhampton Firs did not contain human burials, only votive offerings such as antlers and ox horns. This highlights the diverse symbolic purpose of long barrows, and shows that although Adam's Grave contained several skeletal remains its primary function was to create a striking image of the milk-giving Mother Goddess. A Christian church is a place of reverence and worship yet it also receives the bodies of the dead, the same principal applied to long barrows – Adam's Grave in particular.

During the time of the pagan Saxon incursions into Britain, rivalry existed between the Upper Thames Saxons and the West Saxons, which resulted in a battle in 592 AD between Ceol and Ceawlin called the Battle of Wodnesbeorh (Woden's Barrow). This was the name the Saxons gave to Adam's Grave, the Neolithic long barrow on Walker's Hill. In one of the Saxon chronicles there is a piece of prose which contains the excerpt of a victory song: 'Never, since the English came to Britain, was there a slaughter like the slaughter round the Great Barrow'. The Anglo-Saxon Chronicle for 592 states: 'In this year there was a great slaughter at Wodnesbeorh and Ceawlin was expelled.' Woden or Odin was the one-eyed chief of the Teutonic gods, he was a god of wisdom and war and the son of a giantess. The long barrow will have been deemed sacred by the Saxons which is why they associated it with Woden. Perhaps it was so called because they knew of the existence of the Alton Goddess, and recognized her as being Woden's giantess mother; hence why they named the tumulus on Milk Hill 'white barrow', for it represented the giantess' milk.

A second battle occurred close to Woden's Barrow between Ine King of Wessex and Ceolred of the Mercians in 715 AD. These important battles seem to have had more than just a strategic significance as they both took place on the body of the Goddess. Aubrey Burl estimates that the Wansdyke may have been dug following the first battle on Adam's Grave in 592 AD, but Kenneth Watts says it 'seems likely that it was constructed by the Britons to block Saxon advance from the north in the late fifth century'.[17] The Wansdyke is an enormous linear bank and ditch that stretches from Morgan's Hill to Savernake Forest, and runs across the southern edge of the Marlborough Downs above the Pewsey Vale, passing Tan Hill, Adam's Grave and Knap Hill. On the Wansdyke's long journey across the hills it carefully skirts the Goddess' body, making her part of the territory, for she lies to the south of the defensive earthwork. Could the Alton Goddess have been the religious prize in the territory dispute, and could her existence have influenced the final location of the Wansdyke in the Pewsey Vale? Bonney commented that 'the concentration of Woden names in the vicinity of Wodnesbeorg … has been attributed to the existence of a pagan sanctuary sacred to the god, and perhaps intimately connected with the building of the dyke.'[18] The pagan sanctuary was the Alton Goddess, seen by the Saxons as Woden's giantess mother. They believed that Woden was lying in his grave which was within the bosom of his mother, hence the term 'Woden's Barrow'. Sir James Frazer recorded in his monumental study of comparative religion and world mythology a common funerary belief, which was that 'Mother Earth takes the dead back to her bosom.'[19] This is probably why the Saxons chose to fight at that spot.

Woden's Dyke became the 'Devil's Ditch'[20] yet Woden's Grave was not demonized but christened 'Adam's Grave' by the Church Fathers. By the nineteenth century the barrow was known as 'Old Adam', and a sarsen stone nearby was called 'Eve'. In the Bible, Adam was formed from the 'dust of the earth', defined in the Jewish literature as dust from the Holy Place, from the whole world or even from 'mother earth'.[21] What a fitting name then for the priests to attach to the very Earth Mother herself.

Robert Graves in his seminal work *The White Goddess* explains that Adam, and other figures in the Bible, were usurpers of earlier characters in mythology who were enshrouded in the mystery of the Great Goddess. Other writers also assert that several of the stories in the Bible were modelled from ancient world-wide folklore.[22] Graves claims that the story of Adam and Eve was distorted from an earlier myth featuring a king called Adam: 'The curse in *Genesis* on the woman, that she should be at enmity with the serpent, is obviously misplaced: it must refer to the ancient rivalry decreed between the sacred king Adam and the Serpent for the favours of the Goddess'.[23] The title of the progenitor of mankind has itself arisen from a misinterpretation, for *Adam* is simply the Hebrew word for 'Man'; therefore, originally the character in *Genesis* was known only as 'The Man'.[24] *Adamah* is the Hebrew for 'ground' and *adim* is Sanskrit for 'first' – so the word really means 'the first ancestor of humanity, made from the earth.' In this context Adam's Grave is literally the first grave in the Earth Mother. In Druid mythology one of the many names for the sun was 'A-dda', and the Christian monks associated this with Adam.[25] There is a tantalizing word play with the name A-dda for it also sounds like adder of the snake variety, the traditional English venomous snake. In rabbinic tradition Eve's name, *Havvah*, is associated with the Aramaic *hewyah*, which means 'serpent'.[26] It was said in many old folktales that women are full of serpents, the snakes being the umbilical cord. 'Woden's Barrow' became 'Adam's Grave', whilst Eve (the Alton Goddess) and the huge serpent on Knap Hill lay silently waiting for recognition.

On the extremely steep south side of Knap Hill, overlooking the valley, is a low bowl-shaped barrow that is rather puzzling. Thurnam examined it in the 1800s and reported that 'An opening of at least three yards square, was made in the centre; but excepting some animal bones near the summit, nothing was found after a most careful search.'[27] The Reverend E.H. Goddard suggested that perhaps it was not a barrow.[28] Mrs Cunnington drew the same conclusions: 'The position of this mound on such a very steep hillside seems rather an unusual one for a barrow, and perhaps it was not one at all'.[29]

The strange serpentine bank and ditch that leads down the entire façade of the south side of the hill descends the most precipitous part of the escarpment into the Pewsey Vale, as Goddard questions: 'For what purpose? Too steep for path.'[30] The Cunningtons carried out extensive excavations of Knap Hill in 1908 and 1909. They noticed that the bank emerged from the Neolithic enclosure, followed round the curve of Knap Hill, turned down it and then in a straight line descended 'the very steepest part of the hill, the last few yards being almost precipitous. It ends at the foot of the hill, and if it ever continued over the level ground all trace of it has now been ploughed out.'[31] Mrs Cunnington says that the course of the bank is difficult to follow at close quarters, but at a distance it shows up clearly:

From the road up Alton Hill it can be seen well, and looks like a wide cart track and locally is known as the "Devil's Trackway." Our labourers knew it well by sight, but appeared to think it a kind of optical delusion that vanished at close quarters, and were much interested when the actual bank was pointed out to them. It was suggested that the bank might be merely the result of levelling to make a pathway, possibly down to the nearest water, but the hill is so steep at this point as to make this very improbable, if not indeed impracticable.[32]

Archæologists excavating Knap Hill in 1961 found that, 'The situation has been complicated by a low bank'.[33] The serpentine bank is as mysterious now as it was when it was nicknamed the 'Devil's Trackway'.

The barrow (navel) and serpentine bank (umbilical cord) on Knap Hill, covered with a light dusting of snow.

The umbilical cord that descends the most precipitous part of the Pewsey Vale into the field below.

Researchers have been left to ponder over a causewayed enclosure that shows no evidence of defence, or of being inhabited; a barrow that is not a barrow; and a bank that has no conceivable function. It is only when the hills are viewed as the living body of the Goddess in the landscape that the purpose of the barrow and the bank become apparent. Knap Hill was seen by the Neolithic farmers as the mountainous pregnant belly of the Goddess, a theme that was repeatedly emphasized in the art of that period. The barrow was perfectly positioned to represent her swollen navel, and the bank that has so eluded archæologists is the serpentine umbilical cord that leads directly to the child – the crop of East Field.

A mother and child are connected by the serpentine umbilical cord and for thousands of years the serpent was associated with fertility and childbirth in many cultures. The Dogons of Africa for example believe 'that the snake taught people to give birth. The swallowing rhythm of the serpent compares with the convulsive spasms of birth-giving.'[34] The snake's ability to periodically slough its skin made it a beneficent symbol of rejuvenation and rebirth, and it was therefore intimately linked with the Goddess. The serpent was depicted extensively in prehistoric art, often twining around the belly of the Goddess, or in an anthropomorphic form as a Snake Goddess.

The serpent descends into the mystical underworld to hibernate and then magically re-emerges in the spring: evocative of both the life-force and death. The

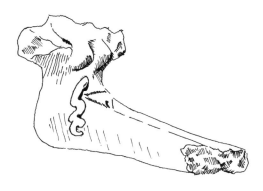

Central Asian goddess figurine with a snake emerging from her womb. The Alton Goddess with the serpentine bank that lies across her stomach displays the same symbolism.

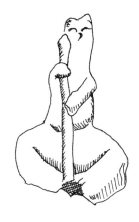

Snake-headed goddess holding the serpent child, 4800 BC.

faience statuette of a High Priestess discovered in a shrine in the Palace of Knossos, Crete, has snakes that coil above and below her waist – symbolic of the heavenly and chthonic aspects of the Goddess. Over her skirt she wears a ceremonial apron which was an emblem of office worn by a priestess of the Mysteries of the Goddess. A girdle is formed by the snakes that encircle her hips, signifying that snakes preside over fertility and childbirth.

The Indian Goddess Kali has a thread called 'Kali's Snake' that represents the umbilical cord,[35] and the Goddess of Alton has a serpentine umbilical cord that winds across her belly (Knap Hill) and leads down to her child – the crops.

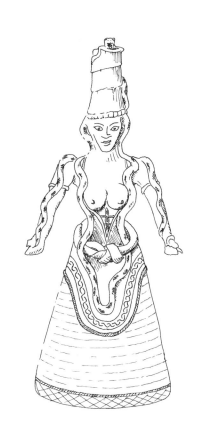

The statuette of a Minoan High Priestess from Knossos, Crete, that is adorned with serpents and a ceremonial apron.
(1600 BC)

Cunnington says that at a distance the bank is clearly visible. This was the whole intention of the Alton Goddess: she was meant to be viewed at a distance so that she could be witnessed in her entirety giving birth to the most important factor in the early farmers' lives.

The very name of the hill that these features were built onto is extremely revealing for although the Saxon word Knap was used to denote a protuberance it can be traced back to the Egyptian word *Cneph* that symbolized the holy serpent and circle. Cneph was an Egyptian deity who held a circle and a serpent and was winged. The word Cneph derives from the Hebrew *ganaph volare* – to fly, a wing.[36] In prehistoric art the Snake Goddess was very often merged with another anthropomorphic figure – the Bird Goddess, and this theme persisted into historic times. The Greek goddess Athena had a snake that flew like a bird, and the winged serpent can be seen throughout world mythology. The words nave and navel are related to Cneph, and thus to the Hebrew 'ganaph', and William Stukeley states that the Teutonic word Knap also derives 'from the Hebrew original.'[37] This is quite astonishing because we have both navel and serpent on Knap Hill!

Linked to the huge serpentine umbilical cord is a natural triangular neck of land to the east of Knap that joins Golden Ball Hill. The shape is important because in ancient art the downward pointing triangle depicted the pubic triangle and vulva of the Goddess, known as the *yoni* in Hindu mythology. All life emerged from the sacred triangle of the Goddess: the Gateway to the Mysteries. The inverted triangle was the symbol of female fertility and rebirth and it was an accentuated feature of the Neolithic figurines.

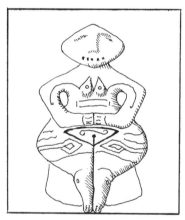

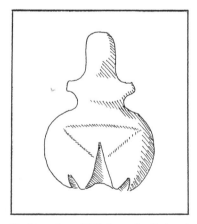

The enthroned Lady of Pazardzik, Bulgaria, c. 4500 BC.

Goddess from Tell Azmak, Bulgaria. These ancient figurines are just two of the many statuettes that are depicted with pronounced pubic triangles — the symbol of female fertility and rebirth: Gateway to the Mysteries of the Goddess.

To the east of the Neolithic causewayed enclosure is an odd triangular-shaped area that the Cunningtons called the plateau enclosure. This occupies the land between Knap Hill and Golden Ball Hill, and is much later in date than the causewayed enclosure because excavations revealed that the plateau ditch had been cut through the silt which had already filled the Neolithic ditch.[38] The pottery retrieved from the site was contemporary with the Late Celtic and Romano-British era. This triangle built onto a triangle is ideally positioned for it is in the spot where the sacred triangle of the Alton Goddess should be. The Celts must have constructed the plateau enclosure to emphasize the natural triangular neck of land that served as the yoni of the Alton Goddess to the Neolithic farmers.

Mrs Cunnington noticed that there were faint traces of ancient tracks underneath the pathway that leads up the eastern side of Knap Hill. She wrote:

'It is thought that the main entrance to the old camp was on this eastern side of the hill to which the trackway leads, as well as that of the plateau enclosure, but the features of the entrance to the old camp have been obscured, if not entirely obliterated, by the later people.'[39] This trackway leads to both the Neolithic and the later Celtic enclosure, and therefore leads to the sacred triangle. To enter each enclosure was to enter through the gates into the Otherworld, or *Annwn* as it was known in Celtic mythology; a ritual entrance into a ritual landscape. The serpentine umbilical cord commences at the south-east corner of the plateau enclosure then comes around the hill and leads straight down to its foot. The reason for this is quite straightforward: the umbilical cord begins at the east coming out of the sacred triangle, then it crosses the belly of the Goddess close to the navel, and descends into the field to the child, the crops.

To add to this picture is a triangular shaped sarsen stone with a hole at its base that was recovered by Nick Riley from the field directly below Knap Hill. Dr Meaden explains that inverted triangular stones were British Neolithic cult objects that portrayed the pubic triangle of the Goddess, and that two of these sarsen stones were found in Wiltshire.[40] The archæologist Marija Gimbutas says that naturally formed, or intentionally carved triangular stones were incorporated into Neolithic monuments.[41] The stone triangles were a focal point for ritual, the ultimate symbol of the Mysteries relating to the underlying cohesion of the ancient Trinity. The inverted triangle has in fact been a constant ritual motif throughout the ages. In Egypt for example, the pharaohs traditionally wore triangular loincloths to reflect the mysteries of the veiled goddess Isis. The ritual attire of members of the Masonic order consists of a square apron with a triangular flap which is worn as an emblem of office, like the apron on the statuette of the Knossos Priestess. The apron denotes that the Mason is a Guardian of the Mysteries and it should ideally be white and unadorned. In this its purest and most potent form the Masonic apron is reminiscent of the sacred triangle of the Goddess, the symbol of rebirth.

Triangular sarsen stone discovered below Knap Hill. Inverted triangular stones were Neolithic cult objects.

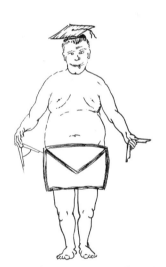

The Masonic Apron with its triangular flap reveals the origins of the Mysteries of Freemasonry.

The triangular sarsen stone found near Knap Hill appears to be a third triangular cult object from Neolithic Wiltshire, and provides further evidence of the existence and exaltation of the Goddess of Alton.

The Neolithic farmers regarded the hills of the Pewsey Vale as the body of a pregnant Goddess who they relied upon to protect their crops. What part did the causewayed enclosure on Knap Hill play in this living landscape, for the archæological evidence attests that it was not a permanent settlement? Aubrey Burl reports that little was discovered at Knap Hill, 'just a few Neolithic sherds under the bank, some local, some from the Cotswolds, flints, some antlers dated to about 3550 BC, one or two animal bones, and it seems that the camp was not occupied for long, maybe was not even finished.'[42] In an account of the excavations of the causewayed enclosure on Windmill Hill, Isobel Foster Smith concludes:

'The camp cannot have been either a permanent settlement or a defensive stronghold; it was a place of assembly where people living elsewhere gathered together during the autumn.'[43] Comparably, at Knap Hill there was evidence of usage, but it wasn't extensive. According to Dyer, Knap Hill's 'skyline position may have made it an ideal place for religious and ceremonial functions'.[44] Knap Hill, like Windmill Hill, was used for ritual purposes. This would explain why 'There was no sign of a fire ever having been lit on the actual floor of the ditch' of the causewayed enclosure.[45] One of the main mysteries of the enclosure is the fact that it appears to be unfinished because it only encompasses half of the hill. The enclosure *is* complete; it was never meant to continue around the south side because it would have defaced the image of the belly, navel and serpentine umbilical cord of the Goddess.

Knap Hill causewayed enclosure.

The Neolithic enclosure on Knap Hill was used as a ceremonial gathering point for the early farmers, and a temporary housing for their animals during the agrarian ritual year. Animals will have been led onto Knap Hill where they could graze on the Goddess and have a degree of protection, being surrounded by banks and ditches that formed corrals. The causeways in the bank could have been a means to separate the livestock. If Knap Hill was used as a temporary animal enclosure then this begs the question – where did the Neolithic farmers live? The ploughed land on Golden Ball Hill was strewn with Neolithic artifacts such as flint flakes and cores.[46] Rather than live their everyday lives on the body of the Goddess the early farmers inhabited the adjacent hill. There was also a Neolithic settlement in the South Field of Alton Priors, formerly known as Burlinch Hill. The settlement has long since been ploughed out, but during drought summers it is conspicuous from the air, displaying evidence of an entrance causeway in the north-east. This spot offers a commanding profile view of the Alton Goddess presiding over the landscape; her vast umbilical cord snaking down to East Field.

At Knap Hill the legendary treasure reputed to be buried there is the Alton Goddess. The giant that emerges when a person runs around Adam's Grave is the giantess in the land. In Alton we have Adam's Grave, Eve and the serpent on Knap Hill. Inside the church at All Cannings, on the south face of the south-west tower pier is a stone carving of a man being bitten by a serpent that coils around his legs.

The carving of a man being bitten by a serpent in All Saints Church, All Cannings. The church was previously dedicated to St Anne.

It seems to be an allegorical carving of the Biblical Adam and the serpent, and perhaps it is echoing the story etched on the hills. The figure of a bishop clad in cape and mitre was inscribed on the font at the church in Avebury. He clutches the Bible to his chest with one hand whilst he wounds a serpent with the crozier in his other hand.

Carving of a bishop pinning a serpent/dragon with his crozier, on the baptismal font in Avebury church.

There is a folktale that snakes could not live within the Avebury Circle, and if any were taken into it 'they immediately died.'[47] There are two stones in the Avebury complex that are nicknamed Adam and Eve – can their story also be told at Avebury?

Avebury is an incredible megalithic complex, one of the most important prehistoric monuments in Europe. Although it is, sadly, a mere shadow of its former glorious self it cannot fail to invoke a sense of wonder, as Sir R.C. Hoare so aptly expressed:

'With awe and diffidence, I enter the sacred precincts of this once hallowed sanctuary, the supposed parent of Stonehenge, the wonder of Britain, and the most ancient, as well as the most interesting relict which our island can produce.'[48]

The vast henge consists of a roughly circular quarry ditch that was originally 33 feet (10 m) deep but is now silted up to half of its former depth. It is surrounded by a chalk bank that encloses an area of 28½ acres (11.5 ha), with four entrances through the bank and ditch. Within the henge are the remains of two adjoining stone circles, surrounded by an outer circle that once consisted of 100 stones. A monolith 21 feet (6.3 m) tall known as the Obelisk once stood in the centre of the South inner circle, and an arrangement of three stones called the Cove stood within the North Circle, of which two still remain. The West Kennet Avenue of parallel sarsen stones runs from the southern entrance of the henge.

It was during a hunting expedition in 1649 that the antiquary John Aubrey 'discovered' Avebury (or Aubury as it was coincidentally called at that time). He believed that it 'doth as much exceed in greatness the so renowned Stonehenge, as a cathedral doth a parish church,' and he made several invaluable notes and plans. Dr Stukeley was inspired by Aubrey's account of Avebury, he paid several visits to the monument in the early 1700s and became fascinated by it. Stukeley witnessed a period of systematic destruction of the stones for building material, or to clear the land for cultivation. The Avebury complex was literally being ravaged before his very eyes, and so on his visits he meticulously recorded the existence of each stone in turn prior to, or during the demolition. From his fieldwork, notes and the accounts of elderly locals he drew the conclusion that the monuments formed the gigantic image of a serpent over several miles of the countryside:

When I frequented this place, as I did for some years together, to take an exact account of it, staying a fortnight at a time, I found out the entire work by degrees. The second time I was here, an avenue was a new amusement. The third year another. So that at length I discovered the mystery of it, properly speaking; which was, that the whole figure represented a snake transmitted through a circle. This is an hieroglyphic or symbol of highest note and antiquity.[49]

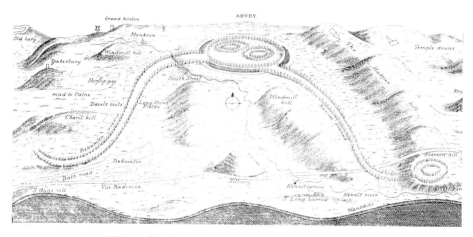

The Avebury Serpent Temple (William Stukeley).

The head of the serpent was a site consisting of concentric circles of stones known as 'The Sanctuary', that stood on Overton Hill until it was demolished in 1724. The West Kennet Avenue created the serpent's neck, and linked the Sanctuary with the Avebury Henge. The henge and outer stone circle were the Holy Circle, and the two inner circles were solar and lunar temples. The tail of the serpent was a second avenue of stones, no longer extant, that ended at Beckhampton.

34

Several archæologists believed that the Beckhampton Avenue never existed and that Stukeley's interpretation was seriously flawed as a consequence. The Beckhampton Avenue was considered to be a fantasy 'until recent excavations proved Stukeley, as in so many of his statements, entirely accurate.'[50]   The majority of the stones of the Beckhampton Avenue had been broken up to build walls, several were buried. We are indebted to Stukeley for he documented stones that have long since vanished, and his notes enabled Mrs Cunnington to rediscover the remains of the Sanctuary in 1930. The theory expounded by Stukeley of the Avebury complex as a huge serpent may at first sight seem whimsical, 'but modern archæology has shown that the original Avebury groundplan was probably much as he drew it'.[51] Of the two hundred stones that once comprised the Beckhampton Avenue there is but one lone survivor. There was also an arrangement of three stones at Beckhampton known as the Cove, of which only one stone remains. These stones have been nicknamed Adam and Eve 'not altogether inappropriately, for their significance is not the origin but the downfall of this serpent-like avenue.'[52]

The Adam and Eve Stones, Avebury.

The carving in the church, and the folktale of serpents being unable to live in the Circle, intimate the Church's subjugation of paganism and its ascendancy over the stone serpent temple of Avebury. The fact that the carving is on the baptismal font highlights the Church's desire to purge the pagan serpent from the heart and soul of its parishioners.

At Avebury, just as at Alton, we have Adam, Eve and Serpent: relatively modern actors in an ancient play that initially featured the Goddess and the Serpent.

CHAPTER FOUR

ALL THE WORLD'S A STAGE

(William Shakespeare)

The Alton Goddess provided a vast stage for prehistoric peoples, but what was the play they performed? The agrarian Neolithic communities were symbiotic with the progression of the seasons, they participated in nature's yearly dramas through ritual and sympathetic magic. The setting and rising of both the sun and the moon during the cycle of the seasons had a deeply symbolic significance to the early farmers. The moon was a visible symbol of the Goddess, periodically changing and growing from Maiden to Mother to Hag. The sun was often seen as male, its corporeal body diurnally disappearing and re-appearing and undergoing an annual death and rebirth. The passage of the sun was marked, as it is today, by the spring equinox, the summer solstice, the autumn equinox and the winter solstice. The equinoxes are when night and day are of equal length and occur in our calendar on March 21st or 22nd (spring equinox), and on or around September 23rd (autumn equinox). The most important festivals of the solar calendar were the summer solstice, the longest day of the year (June 21st), and the winter solstice, the shortest day (December 21st or 22nd). Between the solstices and equinoxes were the cross quarter points that followed the lunar cycle, taking place in early February, May, August and November at the appropriate associated lunar phase. The Celts also observed these lunar quarter days, celebrations began on the eve of the day which involved large festival gatherings on hilltops and the lighting of bonfires. In our present calendar the midpoints between the four solar divisions are fixed dates that occur on February 1st, May 1st, August 1st and November 1st.

In the Pewsey Vale the Neolithic farmers constructed immense stone and earthen props, and the resplendent form of the Alton Goddess was the leading lady in a magical, living play that was enacted with the celestial bodies at the key stations in the ritual year. The seasons of nature reflected the cycles of life and so the play focused on life, death and rebirth and of primary concern was the fusion of the life forces. This was achieved by aligning sites to the lunar quarter days and the solar festivals, particularly the summer solstice.

To prehistoric peoples the summer solstice was the period when the Sun God was at his maximum height and strength. The pagan Celts celebrated the summer solstice by lighting a bonfire and rolling burning wheels down the hillsides to imitate the sun's activities in the heavens. Stonehenge aligns north-east for the midsummer sunrise when the sun's fertilizing rays can be seen to merge with the monument. The sacred triangle of the Alton Goddess faces the midsummer sunrise for it is positioned in the north-east.

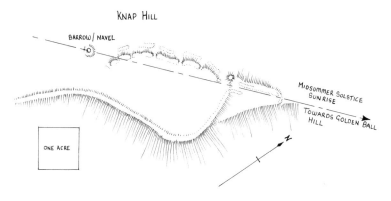

Diagram of the triangular enclosure on Knap Hill that is aligned to the summer solstice sunrise.

In the Neolithic ritual year the summer solstice was the time when the Alton Goddess joined with the Sun God to achieve a mystical conception. From that point onwards the Divine Child would then grow within the womb of the Alton Goddess and at the beginning of August – the midpoint between the summer solstice and the autumn equinox – she would give birth to the harvest child.

The August festival was celebrated on the night of the harvest moon, this was the nearest full moon to the first week in August. It was an ancient belief that the full moon influenced the birth act, and at this crucial time in the agrarian calendar pregnancy and parturition were the themes both on earth, and in the heavens. Michael Dames calculated that at Silbury Hill the reflection of the harvest full moon in the surrounding water of the causeway moat created the miraculous impression of the Silbury Goddess actually giving birth to the moon.[1] This stunning spectacle would have been witnessed by the local Neolithic communities from various hill-top sights in the area.

In the Pewsey Vale, as the August full moon was rising, the Neolithic farmers would have walked in a procession with flaming torches along a prehistoric track from Golden Ball Hill (now called the Tan Hill Way) that leads to the sacred triangle of the Alton Goddess. The procession then continuing across Knap Hill and along the Ridgeway up to the WalkWay Hill breast; then onto Milk Hill and finally to Tan (Ann's) Hill where the celebratory bonfire was held. The fire would not have been lit on her pregnant form but on the neighbouring hill that was not part of her body. Once the solemnities had been fulfilled the Alton Goddess would then deliver the long-awaited child – the harvest.

The August quarter day also featured strongly in the Celtic tradition. In several old Irish texts it was called *Bron Trogain* and the manuscript *Tochmarc Emire* explains that 'Bron Trogain, the beginning of harvest means that the earth sorrows under its fruits. It is a metaphor based on the travail of birth.'[2] The festival was centred around the Earth Goddess and the honouring of the harvest child – her fruits. The very first corn to be cut was given as a propitiatory offering; the belief in Ireland that the fairies claimed the 'tip-top pickle' of the corn derives from this ancient practice.[3] The first fruits were then made into a ceremonial communal feast.

The last sheaf to be harvested was treated with great reverence also because the spirit of the Goddess was thought to reside in it. This belief endured for thousands of years until the change from hand-reaping to mechanized farming. A tradition observed by farmers in many parts of Britain was 'Crying the Neck', the shaping of a handful of the last corn into a bundle that was called the Neck. The oldest reaper held the Neck aloft, and in some areas the farmers would stand around him in a circle and bow to the Neck with their hats removed.[4] In Hone's *Every Day Book* (1826), there is a report of women and men Crying the Neck across the night air in North Devon: 'I heard six or seven "necks" cried in one night, although I knew that some of them were four miles off.'[5] The time-honoured custom of 'Crying the Neck' stems from the distant past, when the Goddess with her elongated neck was revered. The Goddess was often portrayed in New Stone Age art with an extended neck; a composite image consisting of a phallic upper body and the lower half of the body with female characteristics, which highlighted the combination of the life forces.

Goddess figurines with phallus-shaped columnar necks. This dualistic image was a common Neolithic motif. Figurine from Romania, c. 5000 BC. (Above left) Neolithic figurine from Hamangia, Rumania. (Above right)

The Silbury Goddess also has an extended neck-head, and the natural jutting spur from Walker's Hill forms an elongated neck on the body of the Alton Goddess.

The extended 'neck' of the Alton Goddess.

The practice of plaiting a dolly or neck from the last sheaf of corn is archaic, and most probably originated in the Neolithic era. The word dolly derives from 'idol', an object of worship; the early farmers worshipped the Goddess and made countless statuettes of her, and no doubt they made corn images of her at harvest time also. The tradition of making a corn dolly long survived in European folk-custom. If the harvest was late the dolly was called the Corn Mother or the Grandmother, if it was early the figure was known as the Maiden or the Corn Baby:

'If "young", the corn figure was seen as the child that has been delivered from its mother when the sickles cut its cornstalk "umbilical cord".'[6] In Germany the farmers would enact the birth of the harvest child by imitating labour cries and new-born wailing. The woman who had bound the last sheaf played the part of the mother and a boy was the 'baby'.[7] In Lithuania the farmer that cut the last of the rye was called 'the cutter of the umbilical cord'.[8] The Alton Goddess, with her serpentine umbilical cord that leads to the crop of East Field, is a monumental representation of a primordial concept that was once prevalent throughout Europe.

At the end of the harvest the corn dolly was brought home from the field on the processional ride of the last load, a tradition that was widespread throughout England. The horses that pulled the harvest-wain were decorated with garlands, and the dolly was often crowned with flowers. The ceremonial ride of the garlanded dolly is a residuum of Celtic harvest rites. Bishop Gregory of Tours mentions that an image of the goddess Berecynthia was carried around the countryside of Autun, Burgundy, in a processional waggon during the third century AD. The image was covered with a white veil and the people sang and danced before it. The ritual was performed 'for the preservation of their fields and vineyards.'[9] The Roman historian Tacitus recorded a similar practice that was observed by several northern Teutonic tribes who venerated the goddess Nerthus (Mother Earth). Nerthus had a sacred waggon that was covered by a cloth and kept on an island-grove. Every year the image of Nerthus would travel on the consecrated waggon throughout her territory, escorted by a priest. The people would cease all warfare and rejoice in festivities for her presence ensured the fertility of the land.

The umbilical cord of the Alton Goddess that leads to the crops in East Field.

The Alton Goddess joining with the sun in a mystical marriage, and giving birth to the harvest child.

41

The Celtic era saw the emergence of a pantheon of gods. This new breed of hero-gods would often supplant the original goddesses, or they would join with them. The August festival became known as *Lughnasadh* after the Celtic god Lugh. Lugh instituted a great August festival at Teltown in Meath, as a memorial to his foster mother the queen-goddess Tailtiu, who died on this day, and was buried there. Alternative versions of the mythological tradition say that the Lughnasadh festival commemorated Lugh's marriage to the Sovereignty of Ireland, the goddess Eriu.[10] The word Lughnasadh is related to the phrase 'to give in marriage'[11] and Teltown was associated with an ancient form of marriage known as handfasting. Couples were joined in marriage by clasping hands, or simply fingers, through a hole in a gate. The marriage lasted for a year and a day, if after this time the couple wished to dissolve their marriage they would march up two nearby earthen mounds and turn their backs on each other.[12] The practice of temporary marriage continued until the sixteenth century at Teltown, recalling the yearly sacred marriage of the Goddess and the Sun God. William Stukeley described a stone known as the Ringstone at Avebury, 'an odd stone not of great bulk. It has a hole wrought in it.' This stone could well have been the place where handfasting was performed in the Avebury area in prehistoric times, the couple placing their fingers through the hole of the Ringstone. Today only the stump of the stone remains.

The festival of Lughnasadh was called *Hlafmas* or 'loaf-mass' by the Anglo-Saxons, in honour of the sacramental loaf made from the first harvested sheaves of corn. It was Christianized to 'Lammas' but the pagan beliefs endured. Throughout Britain and Ireland the corn dolly was considered to have magical fertilizing powers, and she often presided over the Harvest Home supper. She was then either retained in a barn or the farmhouse until she was fed to the cattle or strewn across the fields the following spring, and in some parishes a communal dolly would sit in the local church.[13]

The medieval harvest traditions are the best reflection of ancient rituals concerning the Goddess, even though they are somewhat attenuated. The Lughnasadh customs were the most difficult to eradicate because farming was a community affair until the mechanization of agriculture, and a good harvest was imperative to all. Halliwell's *Dictionary of Archaic and Provincial Words* records that the term 'Ane' was used in Fitzharbert's *Book of Husbandrie* of 1598 to denote a beard of corn. The primordial name of the Great Goddess who gave birth to the harvest child was still linked with the crops in the sixteenth century!

Saint Anne's Fair that took place on Tan Hill in early August derived from a prehistoric ancestor. An account in the *British Calendar Customs of England* in 1908 reports that people going to St Anne's Fair on Tan Hill had to follow tracks over the Downs that were not used at any other time of the year. This was performed at night, and the pathways were lit with flaming torches.[14] T. Story-Maskelyne also recounts this practice, saying that people travelling to St Anne's Fair followed tracks that were 'ancient British ways leading from near Avebury on the north and from the Stonehenge downs on the south.'[15] The countryfolk travelling to Saint Anne's Fair on Tan Hill were still walking the processional route of the very first farmers in the Pewsey Vale. Máire MacNeill notes that at Mount Brandon in Ireland, the locals would climb the hill on August 1st to celebrate the harvest, and that in the old days the pilgrimage was 'made at dawn. That would mean a night climb or a vigil on the hill.'[16] At Tan Hill this ancient custom was superstitiously still being performed in the 1900s, people only being allowed to tread the sacred paths on Saint Anne's Day – the day that the Neolithic farmers dedicated to Ann the Alton Goddess and her harvest child. Naturally, by this time, the reason for holding the fire at that particular time of the year and on that particular hill was long forgotten; it occurred on Tan Hill because 'it always had done'. Tan Hill Fair is a genuine Neolithic survival, but what is even more remarkable is that in the Pewsey Vale we can also trace the eroded outline of the other prehistoric lunar festivals.

The annual commemorative festival of the dead was a world-wide custom, and in Britain and Ireland it took place on the November quarter day. The festival marked the onset of winter, and the metamorphosis of the Mother Goddess into the Hag. To the pagan Celts the November festival was New Year's Eve or *Samhain*, meaning 'summer's end'; the night when the Druids foretold the future events of the coming year. On Samhain Eve the Old Year ended but the New Year did not begin until the morning, and so the veil between this world and the Underworld was thin, and the spirits of the dead walked abroad. One of the Irish sagas states that the entrances to burial mounds were left open at Samhain, and the interiors were illuminated until the next morning.[17] Offerings of food were laid out for the dead to partake of after their long journey. A sacred bonfire was lit at dusk on local hilltops and all other fires were extinguished, and then rekindled from the ceremonial fire. Blazing torches from the Samhain fire were carried around the fields to purify and bless them, and the surplus livestock were rounded up and killed to provide meat for the winter ahead, from which would be eaten the ceremonial feast.

At this liminal period the sorcerers of the New Stone Age wore masks to identify with the deities and ancestor spirits. This ancient ritual continued in the form of the Hallowe'en custom of guising, whereby villagers in Britain and Ireland would dress in costumes, and wear masks or blacken their faces with soot so that they wouldn't be recognized in the Spirit World. The Guisers would travel from house to house, singing traditional songs and collecting gifts of money and food. In parts of Wales some of the Guisers were masked men dressed in old tatty clothes that were called *gwrachod*, meaning 'hags'.[18] They were obviously impersonating the Hag Goddess that presided over the dead and the winter period.

In County Cork, Ireland, the central character of the November Eve processions was a ritual horse called the *Lair Bhan* (White Mare). The White Mare was a man covered in a white sheet who carried a real horse's skull on a stick. In England this figure was called the Hodening Horse, and also consisted of a man dressed in a sheet wearing a horse's skull who appeared either on November Eve or at Midwinter. On November Eve in Cheshire villages, the Hodening Horse called Wild Horse, or Dick, took part in a house-to-house procession. The people who accompanied Wild Horse sang traditional songs at each house and received gifts in return, whilst the horse chased the young women. He also appeared in a Mummers' play enacted on that night, and following the play the horse's skull was then buried.[19] The Hodening Horse was an important feature of winter festivities in many counties. It was seen to be the harbinger of good fortune and a potent fertility symbol, which is why it chased the young women. The horse was sacred to ancient races because it represented the Spirit of the Solar Year and it was the etheric vehicle that carried the souls of the dead to the Underworld. The psychopompic horse was also believed to possess magical psychic powers. An old Irish manuscript speaks of an oracular horse that would rise out of a hill in County Fermanagh at Samhain and 'tell anyone who asked it everything that would happen to him up to the next Samhain.'[20]   Offerings were left on the hill for the horse until the Church eradicated the pagan practice.

Samhain Eve was replaced by All Saints' Night, or All Hallows' Eve (Hallowe'en). The ancient precepts lingered, however, and the old traditions of Samhain continued to flourish. Candles were lit inside houses or placed on graves to guide the departed home. Offerings of food were laid out on the table, and welcoming fires were kept burning in the hearth all night because the flame, like the sun, was viewed as the very essence of the life force, naturally attracting the souls of the dead to the flame of life. Other elements of the November New Year festival were incorporated into Martinmas, the feast day of Saint Martin, celebrated on November 11th in Britain, Ireland and northern Europe. Martinmas became the time when the cattle were slaughtered and people ate a great feast.

Adjacent to Golden Ball Hill is Martinsell Hill. William Stukeley says: 'I take the name of Martinsal Hill to come from the merriments among the northern people, called Martinalia or drinking healths to the memory of St Martin. There is no doubt about the young people of the neighbourhood assembling here, as they do now upon the adjacent St Ann's Hill upon St Anne's day. At a later time, the people being unwilling to lose a day devoted to pagan rites, such rites were blended with the Christian ceremonies.'[21]

The August harvest rituals occurred on Ann's Hill; the November New Year rituals took place on Martinsell Hill. On Palm Sunday locals would gather on Martinsell Hill, and the youngsters would slide down the hillside on the skulls or jawbones of horses. This strange sport is considered by some researchers to be the 'vestiges of an ancient pagan horse cult'.[22] Palm Sunday eventually became the traditional time for the hill games that had once been held on other festivals. The horse was associated with Samhain in the distant past, and with magical fertilizing powers. Horses' skulls were used to make the eerie heads of the Hodening Horses that were believed to bring blessings to the villages during the winter period. Martinsell Hill's connection with horses' skulls further demonstrates its links with the prehistoric November Eve festival. Sliding the skulls down the hill was a way to ensure the fertility of the land for the coming year.

Prehistoric peoples believed that the sun weakened from Samhain onwards, and that it died in midwinter. The concept of the sun taking refuge within a cave during the winter was widespread in ancient mythology.[23] Caves and long barrows were regarded as wombs of the Goddess and therefore the frail, dying winter sun retired there to be reborn (or resurrected) on December 25th, the old date of the winter solstice. Several Neolithic long barrows are orientated south-east in order to face the midwinter sunrise, the magnificent passage grave of New Grange in Ireland is one such example. It has been suggested that the etymology of New Grange derives from *An Uamh Greine* – the 'Cave of the Sun'.[24] New Grange is aligned to the south-east so that the rays of the midwinter rising sun are admitted through an aperture above the mound's entrance, and along the passageway to illuminate a stone decorated with a triple spiral motif. Adam's Grave long barrow is orientated south-east by north-west, suggesting an alignment with the midwinter sunrise. Perhaps the symbolism at Adam's Grave is that following the death of the old sun the solstice sun child is born out of the darkness, and when it rises on midwinter morn it meets its mother's breast (Adam's Grave), where it rests and is nurtured.

The sun's annual death and revival was a prominent theme in the midwinter Mummers' Plays that were performed in almost every village in England in medieval times. Mummers' Plays are demonstrably pagan in origin, with their roots in the pre-Celtic festivals. The word 'mummer' may have derived from the German *mumme* or the Greek *mommo* which both mean 'a mask'. Mummers were in fact the Hallowe'en Guisers, as November Eve was the beginning of the season when the Mummers' Plays were traditionally performed. From time immemorial people have worn masks and antlers and dressed in animal skins and feathers to invoke aspects of wild nature during magical rites, and to enact the seasonal dramas. There is a striking Palæolithic cave painting at Les Trois Frères, France, of a dancing sorcerer dressed as a stag.

'The Sorcerer' painted on a cave wall at Les Trois Fréres in the French Pyrenees, c. 14,000 BC.

It was traditional for the medieval mummers to wear animal masks, and their costumes were covered with strips of coloured cloth or straw to create a disguise. The identity of the actors had to be concealed so that they were able to transform, like the shamans of old, into the mythological figures they represented.

The words of the Mummers' Plays and the details of the costumes were passed on by an oral tradition. Farmers' lives were inextricably connected with the progression of the seasons and they maintained the customs of their forefathers with great tenacity. Mummers' Plays are a living link with prehistory, reflecting archaic beliefs and rituals performed at the winter solstice. The main plot of the plays was a fight to the death between two key characters, and the resurrection of the dead man by magical means. The duelling characters were a king or Saint George who symbolized light and growth, and a sun-tanned foreigner (Turk) who represented the darkness and decay of midwinter. An eccentric doctor endeavoured to restore the dead man back to life with magic. In some plays the Doctor carried golden pills, or one huge golden pill that represented the sun. The Doctor would succeed in reviving the dead character, and order was then restored. Ralph Whitlock says that the Doctor character was originally 'the Priest or the primitive Medicine-man'[25], the shaman of old. His costume, even in the late 1800s, consisted of wearing feathers.

The actors committed to memory the old words that had been passed on verbally even if they were incomprehensible, so naturally, over the centuries, the plot became confused. In several plays the King slayed the Turkish Knight, but the original storyline consisted of the death and resurrection of the King for he represented the midwinter sun. The words of the Mummers' Play that was performed at Chadlington in Oxfordshire were recorded in 1893; in the play King George says: 'I shed my blood for England's right.' King George then fights with a character called Bullslasher and the King is killed.[26] In several other plays there are direct references to the sun, but it is the King who is mistakingly responsible for the death. Edith Olivier preserved the dialogue of the Mummers' Play from the village of Quidhampton, Wiltshire. In the play King George announces, 'I've cut down my enemies like the evening sun.'[27] In various other plays the words are 'Cut and slain my brother just like the evening sun.'[28]

The concept of the death of the winter sun survived for thousands of years because the narrative line of the folk plays was superstitiously preserved and passed on by generations of farmers. The ambulatory nature of the plays ensured they were a vibrant part of village life, and they also provided an invaluable opportunity for the poor to earn extra money or food during the harsh winter. Farming communities were reluctant to lose touch with their rural past and time-honoured traditions. The following extract from *The Shepherd's Calendar* written in 1827 by John Clare, a Northamptonshire peasant, highlights the countryfolk's need for customs:

Old customs, O I love the sound
However simple they may be,
What ere with time has sanction found
Is welcome and is dear to me. [29]

The winter solstice marked the death and rebirth of the sun to the Neolithic farmers and this theme miraculously prevailed until the late 1800s when the plays began to fall into a decline. The Alton Barnes Mummers' Play was revived by Charlie Ball in the 1930s after he had been taught the script by an old shepherd on the Downs – the place that had formed a vast stage to the Neolithic and Celtic farmers.

At the winter solstice the sun was reborn, and on the February quarter day prehistoric peoples celebrated the earliest signs of the earth's renewal as lambs were born, and flowers and catkins began to appear. Livestock were moved to high pastures at this period and the festival was associated with breastfeeding because the ewes were lactating. The Celts called the February quarter day *Óimelc*, or *Imbolc* (both pronounced imelk) meaning 'ewe's milk'. The most appropriate spot in the Pewsey Vale to celebrate Óimelc – the pastoral festival associated with breastfeeding – was undoubtedly Milk Hill. On Milk Hill and Adam's Grave the livestock could be nourished from the very breasts of the Alton Goddess.

The first stirrings of spring heralded the transformation of the Crone to the radiant Maiden. In the pagan Celtic religion Óimelc was associated with the multifarious maiden goddess Brigid/Bride – patroness of healing, poetry, crafts and fertility. Brigid was cognate with Brigantia, the goddess of the northern Romano-British tribes, and in Irish mythology she was the daughter of a prominent god called the Dagdha. The auspicious return of the hibernating serpents occurred on her Feast Day, and in the Scottish Isles effigies of snakes were made to symbolize this.[30] She also protected cattle, and her aid was sought by women in childbirth.

The attributes of the goddess Brigid were transferred by the Christian Church to Saint Brigid, who supposedly founded a convent at Kildare in Ireland in 490 AD. Saint Brigid's holy day February 1st was the old Óimelc festival. There is very little evidence that Saint Brigid was a true historical figure, indeed the details of her birth indicate she was of supernatural origin; the saint was the goddess Brigid reinvented by hagiographers. Saint Brigid was born at sunrise, her mother standing with one foot on the threshold which meant that she was born 'neither within nor without the house', a common motif in Celtic mythology. She lived with a druid and was fed on the milk of a white cow with red ears, an animal from the Otherworld. At Saint Brigid's convent in Kildare nineteen nuns kept a perpetual fire burning that no male was allowed to approach. The Gaelic name of the convent is *Cill Dare* (Church of the Oak) which indicates that it was originally a pagan sanctuary. The nuns who tended the sacred fire were continuing a ritual that had previously been performed by nineteen Druidesses, the number nineteen probably symbolizing the moon's 18.6 year cycle through the heavens.

Saint Brigid was known as 'Christ's Milkmaid' and she was also the protectress of cattle. The milk from her cows was so copious that it formed a vast lake across the land. Her association with fire, with cattle, and particularly with a flowing abundance of milk, are all aspects of the Celtic fire festival that celebrated the lactation of the ewes. Shamrocks and flowers were said to spring up wherever St Brigid walked. This again is an attribute of the Goddess who is no longer the Hag of winter but the harbinger of spring – the Maiden. An old Scots Gaelic saying recalls this ancient belief:

> Bride put her finger in the river
> On the Feast Day of Bride
> And away went the hatching mother of the cold.[31]

Brigid was invoked at springs and wells at Óimelc, where people would leave offerings, and drink the waters that were believed to be particularly imbued with curative and fructifying powers at this time. Numerous holy wells and springs throughout Britain and Ireland were dedicated to Brigid/Bride. At Glastonbury in Somerset there is a carving of Saint Bride milking a cow on the entrance arch of Saint Michael's Tower on the Tor. A mound at nearby Beckery is called Bride's Mound and there was once a holy well there connected with a spring called St Bride's Well. A community of women are reputed to have lived on Bride's Mound and, like the nuns at Kildare, they kept an ever-burning fire in St Bride's honour. There is a spring in Westbury, Wiltshire, called Bridewell Springs and no doubt this was dedicated to Bride. The spring in Alton Priors is known as the Broad Well. On an Anglo-Saxon charter it was recorded as *BradeWyll*, a probable corruption of BrideWell. All Saints

The springs at Alton Priors.

Church in Alton Priors was built close to the springs, and under a trap door in the church is a holed sarsen stone; an old name for sarsens in Wiltshire is 'Bridestone'. Perhaps Bride was invoked at the springs in Alton Priors during the Óimelc celebrations.

The Church replaced the pagan festival with Candlemas (February 2nd), the Feast of the Purification of the Virgin Mary, to mark the opening of spring. Candlelit processions were observed which were directly inherited from the Roman festival that honoured the goddess Februa, when candles were carried through the streets. Candlemas was also reminiscent of the ancient fire festival that the Celts associated with the goddess Brigid.

It has been possible to reconstruct the rituals that took place in the Vale of Pewsey on the summer solstice, Lammas, Samhain, the winter solstice and Óimelc. There is one final lunar festival that has not yet been addressed – the May quarter day known as *Beltane*. In the farming year this was a period when there was an abundance of grass and so the herds were turned out to pasture. The presence of flowers and greenery at this time indicated the blossoming fertility of the Earth Goddess which was cause for joyous celebration. The festival began at moonrise on Beltane Eve and it marked the beginning of summer. The word Beltane is thought to derive from the Celtic *bel taine* meaning 'bright fire' which refers to the lighting of the sacred bonfire on a hilltop. A ninth-century Irish churchman called Cormac recorded in his *Glossary* that all other fires were extinguished at this time, and the Druids lit the Beltane bonfire whilst chanting spells. Often two separate fires were lit which the cattle were driven between to protect them from disease. In later survivals of the Beltane rituals in Wales, nine men would empty their pockets of iron and money and gather sticks from nine different trees. The sticks were then laid crosswise inside a circle that had been cut out of the ground and the fire was kindled with them.[32] This is clearly a genuine survival from the Celtic era for nine was a mystical number to the Celts. The men removed iron from their pockets because they wished to invoke the aid of the fairies, and it was a common belief that fairies are afraid of iron.

The rites performed at Beltane were to promote fertility and to assist the growth of livestock, crops and the sun. The sacred bonfire was the very essence of the sun on earth. In Ireland a man who was due to marry would leap across the flames in order to purify himself. When the Beltane fire was low pregnant women would step through it to ensure a safe delivery, and children were carried across the ashes to bless and protect them. Women and men would dance *deosil* or 'sun wise' around the fire. In Scotland, Beltane cakes or bannochs were rolled down the hillsides as 'a magical imitative act, symbolising and aiding the course of the sun.'[33] A game was played at Beltane which involved a golden ball and a decorated hoop. Paddy Slade writes:

The meaning of this game is lost in antiquity. The golden ball seems to be a straightforward fertility symbol; other sources say that it represents the sun passing through the heavens. Two people pick up a large, decorated hoop and throw a golden ball to someone on the other side. It is very unlucky to drop the ball, or fail to get it through the hoop.[34]

The adjoining hill to Knap is called Golden Ball Hill which is a 'mystery to place-name experts'.[35] Some writers have suggested that the hill derived its name from the yellow rock rose – *Helianthemum vulgare* – that was once prolific across the Downs but is now only present on Knap Hill.[36] This is highly unlikely because the rock rose was not merely specific to Golden Ball Hill and it no longer grows on that particular hill. Could Golden Ball Hill have been the place where the Beltane rituals were performed in the distant past, namely, the golden ball game? The Alton Goddess is connected to Golden Ball Hill by her sacred triangle in the east; to pass a golden ball through a hoop and down the side of the adjacent hill would have been an act of sympathetic magic designed to encourage the sun to impregnate her outstretched form at the summer solstice.

According to a nineteenth-century report, a special ball game was traditionally played at the nearby Martinsell Hill on Palm Sunday: 'They take their positions at intervals in a line from the base of the hill to its summit, and using hockey sticks knock the ball in succession up the hill until it reaches and passes the summit.'[37] In addition to this ball game, 'Oranges were thrown down the slopes and boys went headlong after them.'[38] At first sight these hill-games seem to be nothing more than mere amusement, but as H.W. Timperley points out in *The Vale Of Pewsey*, they are thought to have originally been something more significant than national holiday pastimes, although this is what they eventually became:

It is probable that they were as old as the earthworks on the hilltops and were just as much the remains of the people who made the earthworks, that in the beginning the games were, in fact, festivals of a pagan religion in which the fertility of cultivated earth and domesticated animals were set above all else.[39]

The game of throwing oranges down the hillside appears to be a confused remembrance of the Beltane golden ball ritual originally carried out on Golden Ball Hill, the oranges symbolising the sun. The hockey stick game was also significantly connected with Beltane. A Roman pottery mould discovered in Kettering, Northamptonshire, and the plaques on ritual crowns from Hockwold in Norfolk depict naked players that are holding a hooked stick and balls.[40] H.J.M. Green says that they are suggestive of a religious ceremony rather than a leisure activity: 'It is possible that in its origins the rite is sympathetic magic to ensure the passage of the sun across the heavens.'[41] The hockey game and the orange game were mistakenly performed on the neighbouring Martinsell Hill, for all that had survived in folk memory was the rolling of a golden ball down the hills – the oranges and hockey sticks were the last vestiges of the archaic Beltane fertility rite. Golden Ball Hill was inhabited by the Neolithic farmers, who would have rolled burning fire brands down the hillside to assist the sun's growth so that it would be strong enough, at the summer solstice, to join with the fully fecund Goddess. The origin of the name of Golden Ball Hill need no longer be an enigma when the Alton Goddess and the traditions surrounding her are taken into account.

Beltane eventually became known as May Day and the fertility of the Goddess and the growth of the Sun God continued to be the underlying themes of the festival. The word May comes from the Latin *Maius*, thought to be derived from Maia, the Roman goddess of Spring.[42] In Scandinavia the month of May is dedicated to Maj, the Maiden.[43] Gangs of boys would sound horns at dawn on May morning to announce the arrival of summer. Young girls went out before sunrise to wash in the May morning dew for it was believed to have healing and beautifying properties. Aubrey noted in his *Natural History of Wiltshire* that a man named William Gore, of Clapton in Wiltshire, used to walk through the May dew to cure his gout.[44] People collected leaves, flowering hawthorn known as 'the may', and blooms from the woods in order to decorate their homes and to make garlands that were carried in the May Day processions. Villagers decorated the maypole and gaily skipped around it. This practice stems from archaic fertility rites and the worship of trees: the earliest maypoles were trees that had been brought in from the woods, stripped of their branches and erected on the village green. The local community danced around the maypole which was the *axis mundi*, the centre around which the world revolved.

A salient figure in the May Day festival was the May Queen, a young girl dressed in white and crowned with a garland of flowers. She sat on a throne and was carried in procession. The May Queen is reminiscent of the youthful Maiden Goddess who presided over spring. In some villages the May Queen wasn't an elected girl but a doll seated in the centre of a garland. A group of young people told an enquirer at Bampton in Oxfordshire that the doll in their May garland was 'a goddess'.[45] In the Isle of Man a ritual battle was enacted between the Queen of May and her attendants, and the Queen of Winter and her attendants. The Queen of May and her followers were girls dressed in 'the gayest and best manner', and the Queen of Winter and her entourage were men dressed in women's winter clothing. The two groups would engage in a mock battle and the Queen of Winter would attempt to imprison the Queen of May.[46] This May Day custom is an echo of the ancient sacred drama of the Winter Hag shapeshifting into the Spring Maiden.

The May Queen was sometimes accompanied by a May King; as a pair they conducted the May games and were also known as the Lord and Lady of the May, or Robin Hood and Maid Marian. A curious dancing figure called Jack-in-the-Green also took part in the May Day processions in England. The Jack was a man encased in a large hollow wicker-work frame down to his ankles, which was completely covered with leaves and green branches so that only his eyes were visible. The Leaf King of Hanover and the Green George of Russia, Rumania and Transylvania are Jack-in-the-Green's counterparts.[47]

Jack-in-the-Green entered into the iconography of the medieval Christian churches in Britain and parts of Europe in the form of a foliate head. The foliate head or 'Green Man'[48] consists of a human face entwined with leaves that sprout from the mouth, ears or nostrils. The motif first appeared in the form of a leaf mask in Roman art in the first century AD that was carved in temples and on sarcophagi.[49] There are isolated examples of foliate heads in the Christian Church dating from the fourth century, and in the late Middle Ages the Green Man was an extremely popular motif in church architecture – adorning fonts, rood screens, roof bosses, corbels and even the tombs of various saints. The Green Man's penetrating eyes peer from within a leafy canopy like the Jack-in-the-Green of the May festivities. Several of the Green Man carvings in churches are hawthorn masks: a beautiful example dating from the fourteenth century can be found at Sutton Benger, Wiltshire.

The Green Man in the church at Sutton Benger consists of hawthorn, the tree associated with the May Day festivities.

Hawthorn was the may-blossom and some of the foliate heads are depicted wearing crowns, therefore the May King, the Green Man and Jack-in-the-Green are different expressions of a pre-Christian archetype – the Guardian of the Greenwood.

The Green Man was a personification of the consort of the Goddess who, like the sun, underwent a yearly death and rebirth. The foliate head is Jack-in-the-Green in his death aspect, which is why the majority of the carvings depict him as morose and sorrowful. His eyes stare with a sense of foreboding and he is often portrayed with a lolling tongue as though the branches are choking him; he has no body, only a head. The oracular severed head was a common theme in Celtic mythology, present in such tales as the medieval poem *Sir Gawain and the Green Knight*, and the story of the god-king Bran the Blessed whose severed head spoke for many years. This stems from the world-wide myth of the vegetation god or king who elected to die each year, usually by decapitation, and was miraculously restored to life. His death ensured that the land was replenished. John the Baptist was also decapitated, he prepared the way for Christ who chose to die in order to save humanity, and was subsequently resurrected.

In the tale of Sir Gawain and the Green Knight, the New Year festivities at Camelot are interrupted by the dramatic entrance of a gigantic, fearsome knight who is 'bright green all over' and wielding a huge axe. This imposing figure offers a challenge to the knights of the court: any knight present can cut off his head providing the knight agrees to his own decapitation a year later. The gallant Sir Gawain accepts the challenge and strikes a deadly blow to the Green Knight's neck with the almighty axe. To the utter amazement of the court the headless knight stands, picks up his head, and his mouth instructs Gawain that he must journey to the Green Chapel in exactly one year's time and receive a blow to the neck in return. The Green Knight then mounts his horse and rides out of Camelot.[50] The Green Knight, Jack-in-the-Green and Robin Hood clad in green apparel are all symbolic of springtime vegetative resurgence: they are the Green Man in his aspect of resurrection.

The Corn Jack Mummers on Silbury Hill celebrating the resurrection of Jack-in-the Green at the spring equinox.

A fair used to be held in Marlborough in May called Jacky John's Fair. People would meet in the meadows near the River Og and then join hands and dance through Marlborough up to the town hall and back to the meadows. Before returning to Jacky John's Fair the people that had participated in the processional dance threw offerings into the river. The dance they performed was a version of 'Threading the Needle' in which two people lead making an arch with their arms and the other dancers pass under the arch in couples. The last couple form a new arch and the dance continues.[51] Ralph Whitlock says that folklorists regard 'Threading the Needle' as 'a very ancient dance of sacred origin, performed at the time of a pre-

Christian spring festival.'[52] The Pewsey Vale and surrounding area has amazingly conserved, albeit in a diluted form, the myths and seasonal rites from the Neolithic era.

Grasping the tattered fragments of the original Neolithic script we can see that following the Beltane festival the fertile Maiden, clothed in a green mantle, is ready for union again with the Sun God at the summer solstice. And thus: 'The wheel is come full circle' (*King Lear* Act 5 Sc 3), and the curtain rises for the seasonal performance. The Goddess gives birth once more to the harvest child, and with the onset of winter the Crone silently shuffles onto the stage to give the crowning performance. This is the most mysterious aspect of the entire drama and one that deserves greater attention.

CHAPTER FIVE

THE HAG OF SILBURY HILL

I am a hill: where poet's walk

From the *Song of Amergin*
(trans. Robert Graves)

The Hag who presided over winter, the season of disintegration, darkness and death is the most enigmatic aspect of the Triple Goddess. We have seen how Neolithic cultures placed great emphasis on the propitiation of the maternal aspect but the Crone was also represented in prehistoric art. Marija Gimbutas categorized Neolithic depictions of the Hag as 'stiff nudes'. She describes ugly-looking figurines found in fifth millennium BC graves in Varna, East Bulgaria, whose strange heads resemble 'the dishevelled hair of an Old Hag; they seem to be replicas of winter corn dolls.'[1] A limestone figure was discovered in a Neolithic long barrow in Notgrove, Gloucestershire. It had been placed on the roof of the chamber complex so it was obviously of symbolic significance; this natural stone markedly resembles a hooded hag.[2]

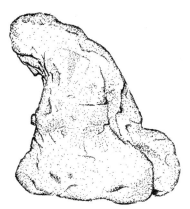

The limestone figure of a hag that was discovered in the Neolithic chambered long barrow at Notgrove, Gloucestershire.

A flint offering that resembles a hooded hag was found in the west chamber of West Kennet long barrow.

Michael Dames recognized that the image of a hooded hag goddess can also be seen in a votive flint offering that was retrieved from the west chamber of West Kennet long barrow.[3] Thurnam noticed that the flint had been 'elaborately chipped at the edges'[4]

Silbury Hill is a monumental image of the Mother Goddess who was associated with summer, and the ripening of crops. Towards the end of summer there is heavy surface evaporation over the chalk downs near Silbury, causing the River Kennet and its source the Swallowhead spring to dry up and disappear. The waters magically re-appear in February coinciding with the first signs of spring, and the return of the Maiden. Stukeley recorded that the old name for the river was Cunnit,[5] which derives from the Middle English *cunte*; the Swallowhead/Cunnit confluence was thus seen as the maidenhead of the youthful goddess of spring. The principal Roman town in the Kennet valley was called 'Cunetio', which affirms the antiquity of the

Aerial view of Silbury Hill and a gigantic spectral hag. © Crown copyright. NMR.

The Hag Goddess overlooks the Silbury Mother Goddess. © Crown copyright. NMR.

name 'Cunnit'. The River Winterbourne that joins the Kennet at Silbury is intermittent, so as its name suggests it tends to flow only in the winter. The Winterbourne creates a miraculous image in the wintertime – that of a huge hag.

How can this be possible? Is it simply a simulacrum, a likeness formed by a quirk of nature, or could the water from the Winterbourne have been utilised in some way to form an artificially constructed image of a hag?

This mysterious hag is comprised entirely of trenches and a large curving ditch that delineates her back. There is no doubt that these are in fact artificial ditches and not simply natural watercourses, for that specific area is noted as a water meadow. Water meadows have been described as 'a jewel of British agriculture' and are, in the main, a product of the south and south-west. T. Davis writing about farming methods in Wiltshire says: 'There is, perhaps, no part of this kingdom, where the system of watering meadows is so well understood, and carried to so great perfection, as in this district.'[6] Water meadows were created in order to enrich the soil for the provision of an early, vital flush of grass for sheep to eat, at a time when hay was scarce. They consist of a series of parallel beds and channels that divert water from a nearby river in a regulated manner, on and off the land. The majority of water meadows are believed to have been constructed in the seventeenth century, and those dating from that period differ greatly in design from the water meadow at Silbury. Seventeenth-century water meadows have a complex carrier system, whereas the ditches and trenches at Silbury are rudimentary, and seem to deliberately mark out the shape of a hag figure. The questions of why and by whom immediately spring to mind but research into water meadows does present difficulty, for as George Atwood states: 'The origin and early history of our English water-meadows is very obscure.'[7]

Previous pastoralists have experimented with controlling water in meadows: there are water meadows on the Gloucestershire Churn and the Hampshire Avon that date from the Roman period.[8] The antiquarian John Aubrey says that the Roman poet Virgil born in 70 BC wrote about water meadows,[9] Virgil himself being the son of a prosperous farmer. Were the Romans the pioneers in water meadow construction? Where did the idea of water meadows originate? T. Davis succinctly provides the answer to this question in the *General View of the Agriculture of the County of Wiltshire*, 1794:

The idea of watering meadows, so far as it relates to bringing the water *upon the land,* was taken from *nature.* It must have been always observed, that winter floods produced fertility, provided the water did *not* remain *too long* on the land. The idea of taking the water *off* the land *at will,* and bringing it *on again at will,* is the effect of *art;* and the knowledge of the proper time to do this, the effect of observation.[10]

The Neolithic farmers went to great lengths to construct Silbury Hill and its surrounding ditch in order to convey a deeply artistic and spiritual message: the ditch providing the icing on the conceptual cake for it enabled the retention and control of water. With this in mind it is not inconceivable that Neolithic, or Celtic farmers, could have created the crude ditches that form the Silbury Hag – their vision gleaned from the observation of nature.

In 1996, Wessex Archæology carried out an archæological evaluation of part of the water meadow area around Silbury, prior to Southern Electric laying a power cable trench. In the report of their findings the archæologists concluded:

'The presence of waterlain silt deposits down to at least 1.5 m below current ground level in certain areas indicated that in both pre-Roman and post-Roman periods this area experienced very wet conditions, probably with seasonal flooding from the River Winterbourne to the east.'[11] This evidence indicates that the area was already a flood plain in the Neolithic era, and therefore early agriculturalists could have dug out the ditches to control this seasonal flooding if they had wanted to create pastureland. Professor Dimbleby's findings following a detailed analysis of the environmental material from the 1967 excavations at Silbury, demonstrate that the Neolithic farmers were indeed using the area for pastureland:

The absence of cereal pollen and weeds of bare soil suggest that arable farming was not being practised in the immediate vicinity. Among the macroscopic plant remains on the old land surface the leaves of the grasses could be recognised; they still had some green colouration when first excavated. It was noticed that the leaves were square-ended, not pointed, suggesting that they had been grazed by stock.[12]

The weed pollen also contained large amounts of ribwort plantain which is found in pastureland.

The Hag Goddess of winter almost disappears during summertime.

The Silbury Hag had a dual function – to provide an early bite for animals, and to convey a deeply symbolic message, for the ditches were designed to retain water so that during the winter floods the hag's body would be clearly visible. The winter windswept snow collecting within the trenches would also highlight the hag's features. The Silbury Hag is barely discernible during the dry summer months which is quite appropriate because this is the period that is associated with the Silbury Mother Goddess.

The creation of the Silbury Hag was extremely ingenious and she must surely have been appreciated from somewhere other than the air. The nearby Waden Hill provides the ideal viewing spot, and the hill's name derives from the Anglo-Saxon *Weadhun*, meaning 'place of pagan worship'.[13] The hooded 'flint hag' that was discovered in the west chamber of West Kennet long barrow appears identical to the Silbury Water Meadow Hag. If this piece of flint was intentionally placed within West Kennet long barrow to represent the Silbury Hag opposite, then this is an indication that her designers were in fact the Neolithic people; however, this flint hag is merely one tiny piece of the Silbury Hag jigsaw.

There is another possible clue as to the identity of the Hag's designers – the two egg-shaped pools that adjoin her vast body. These pools undoubtedly play a role in the overall symbolic message of the Silbury Hag, so what could their function be? The egg was a perennial feature in Neolithic art, it was painted on pottery and incorporated into the design plan of chambers for the dead. The egg represents new life, regeneration, and in prehistoric art it is often linked with water. The egg is the same colour as bone so it is connected with death and rebirth, and interestingly

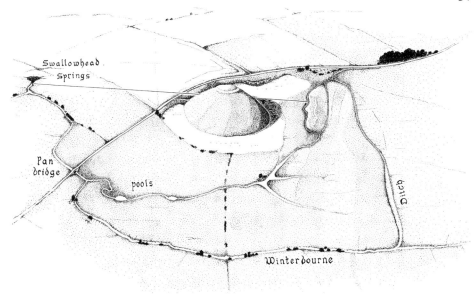

The Silbury Trinity – the maiden springs, the mountain mother and meadow hag.

Gimbutas recognized that the symbols associated with the Hag, the goddess of Death ranged 'from bare bones to eggs and uteri'.[14] The Silbury Water Meadow Hag with her egg-shaped pools seems to epitomize the Winter Hag Goddess of Death and Regeneration that featured in the lives of the Neolithic culture.

At Silbury the rivers, the hill and the water meadow form an harmonious poetic and religious message of the Trinity – the Maiden, the Mother and the Hag. The Water Meadow Hag's eye is in alignment with the edge of the Silbury Mother and with the Swallowhead spring – the maidenhead, connecting all three aspects.

A custom that was observed by locals every Palm Sunday until the mid-nineteenth century was the ascent of Silbury Hill, upon which they would eat figs and cakes, and drink water that had been fetched from Swallowhead spring. Figs are symbols of fertility, and this tradition at Silbury was probably the survival of a prehistoric ritual associated with the Goddess: the water from the maidenhead being taken to the summit of the Silbury Mother.

It is evident from the construction of the Silbury Hag that the Winter Crone figure played a crucial role in the spiritual lives of her designers, and to explore this in more depth we must look to early folklore sources.

It is within the rich tapestry of Celtic mythology that we are able to glimpse the face of the enigmatic Hag-deity that is beneath the hood. The tales of Celtic times were preserved by the Bards who were required to commit to memory hundreds of poems, stories and songs. These awesome poets were literally walking libraries: entire volumes of ancestral lineage, ancient history, rites and legends were deposited within their minds. Medieval monastic scholars in Ireland and Wales recorded fragments of this oral tradition in various manuscripts. Ireland in particular retained many elements of ancient rituals and legends, preserving customs that had long since vanished in other parts of Europe. Ireland is, therefore, a repository of myth and history, and in analyzing its legends we can access rituals and beliefs that were once pervasive in Britain.

The sovereignty of Ireland was personified as a goddess in the Irish mythological tradition, and the sacred marriage of the king-elect with the deified sovereignty of the land was a central theme. It was imperative for the future king to mate with the Goddess in her hag aspect so that the sovereignty of Ireland could be conferred on him, and to ensure that his reign was blessed. Anne Ross writes:

'the goddess appears to the future king, and as a rule to his two brothers, in the form of a hideous old woman; the brothers reject her sexual advances with horror. The one who is to be king, however, accepts them, and thereupon the hag turns into the most lovely girl imaginable.'[15] This clearly displays the power that the Hag was believed to hold in Celtic times, and illustrates the continuance of the Neolithic concept of the Trinity for the hideous hag that appears in the tales can easily shape-shift into the beautiful maiden.

In the legends of King Arthur there is a story of the gallant Sir Gawain marrying a hag. King Arthur travelled to High Hesket, Cumbria, to seek out a gigantic knight who had supposedly wronged a woman and her husband. The enchanter-knight told the king that he had a year and a day to answer the question, 'What is it that a woman most desires?' If Arthur did not give the correct answer then he would die. Arthur and his knights scoured the land collecting answers to the riddle, and when the time came he set off to meet the knight. Arthur saw an old woman on his journey who told him she knew the true answer, but she would only reveal it if one of his noble knights promised to marry her. Sir Gawain pledged that he would become her husband and in return the hag saved Arthur's life by informing him of the answer to the riddle which was: 'That which a woman most desires is to have her will.' The hideous hag married Sir Gawain and on their wedding night she requested a kiss. Despite his dread the knight bent down, and after kissing her on the lips he discovered that the hag was transfigured: the most beautiful maiden in the land stood there before him and King Arthur's knights rejoiced.

A theme that is recurrent in the vernacular mythic literature of Britain and Ireland is that of the Hag who possesses great wisdom. A fourteenth-century Welsh volume called *The Book of Taliesin* consists of a corpus of tales, poems and songs that are attributed to a bard known as Taliesin (pronounced *tal-yes-in*), who was the 'Primary Chief Bard of the Island of Britain'. Taliesin was a sixth-century bard, yet many of the poems said to have been composed by him actually pre-date him by hundreds of years and belong to the Celtic mythological tradition. John Matthews explains that the works were attributed to Taliesin because he was 'a representative figure who spoke for the ancient mystery religion of the native British people.'[16] In several of the poems Taliesin is an apotheosized character, and in the story of Taliesin's birth a hag goddess known as Caridwen or Ceridwen plays a crucial role.

Ceridwen's son Afaggdu, also known as Morfran, was so ugly that she believed she had to empower him with wisdom in order for people to accept him. She resolved to achieve this task by brewing a potion in her magical cauldron. The mixture had to boil for a year and a day so she instructed the servant boy Gwion to watch over the cauldron and tend the fire. Three precious drops of Inspiration splashed onto Gwion's thumb and the pain from the scald was so intense that he thrust his thumb into his mouth to soothe it. The gift of poetic enlightenment intended for her son was subsequently bestowed upon Gwion; the cauldron then burst in two and the waters flowed from it into a nearby stream. Ceridwen was so enraged when she returned that she pursued Gwion, and he changed himself into a hare to escape from her. Ceridwen transformed into a greyhound, so Gwion ran to the river and metamorphosed into a fish. Ceridwen changed into an otter and swam after him, forcing Gwion to turn into a bird. Ceridwen became a hawk, and just as she was about to swoop upon him he turned himself into a grain of wheat. He could not outmanoeuvre the hag, however, because she instantly became a hen and then swallowed him. Nine months later Gwion was reborn, he was so beautiful that Ceridwen could not bear to kill him so she set him adrift on the sea inside a leather bag. A nobleman called Elphin discovered the child and called him Taliesin ('Radiant

Brow'), and he became the ultimate shaman and Primary Chief Bard of Britain. Here we witness the Hag as the initiator of Gwion, forcing him to transform many times. She is the tutor pushing her apprentice through all of creation; she is the predator and he is forced to use his wits and transform into a creature of the land, sea and sky until he attains the level required of a bardic-seer.

Similarly, in *Cormac's Glossary*,[17] there is the story of the master-poet named Senchan who travelled to the Isle of Man with an ugly youth in order to search for a famous lost poetess. When they arrived they met an old woman on the shore who offered to assist them, providing Senchan answered a poetic riddle. She recounted one half of a poem and invited Senchan to complete it, but as he hesitated the ugly youth supplied the answer. After the contest the ugly youth disappeared, the old woman was recognised as the missing poetess, and Senchan returned with her to Ireland. There they met the hideous youth who had become a handsome hero. In both of these tales the transformation from youth to refined poet is instigated by the cunning crone who is the well spring from which all poetic wisdom flows. This theme extends through to Saxon times for in the Viking Prose Edda there is a long story in which the mighty thunder god Thor faces several trials, the last being a contest of strength with a hag. Thor had to wrestle with the hag but was incapable of moving her at all. The hag forced Thor down onto his knees, and the king then ordered the fight to end. The story is an allegory of the fact that Old Age and Death overcome the strongest of men, and that Thor and his companions had insufficient wisdom to conquer fate.[18]

A clearer picture is beginning to emerge of who the Hag Goddess was – divine, wise, the tutor of many heroic gods, bestower of sovereignty and keeper of the Cauldron of Inspiration and Knowledge, who was but one face of the Triple Goddess as she could easily shapeshift into the maiden aspect, or any animal. In the *Book of Lismore* there is a story of a board game that was played by the boys of Rome, featuring a hag at one end of the board and a maiden at the other:
'The hag lets loose a dragon while the maiden releases a lamb; the lamb overcomes the dragon. When asked why they played this game the boys said it had been taught to them by the Sibyl. The truth behind this concerns a cosmological struggle in which the transformation of hag into maiden is seen as a battle.'[19] These facets are typified by the Morrigán of the Irish tales: a Celtic battle Goddess who appears as a hag or a maiden, or as a crow or raven. The crow connection is interesting because the word crone derives from 'carogne, carrion' – the carrion crow being the common European crow. Prehistoric figurines of the Hag Goddess often portrayed her with bird-like features. The Morrigán was a fearsome hag who appeared to warriors and influenced battles.

A motif that frequently occurs in Celtic mythology is that of the spectral washer-at-the-ford: a hag who is washing the blooded clothing of those destined to die in battle. Here we notice the Hag's connection with water, with prophetic wisdom, and with death, although her presence is somewhat less benign where death is concerned than in the Neolithic era due to the Celts being a warrior nation. The following extract from a poem written by William Sharp (pen-name Fiona Macleod) conjures up the awesome image of the washer-at-the-ford:

A shadowy shape of cloud and mist, of gloom and dust, she stands,
The Washer of the Ford:
She laughs, at times, and strews the dust through the hollow of her hands.
She counts the sins of all men there, and slays the red-stained horde—
The ghost of all the sins of men must know the whirling sword
Of the Washer of the Ford.[20]

The pages of the early mythic literature abound with hags who are often referred to as Cailleachs. The word Cailleach literally means old woman, hag or crone and is linked with the word *caille* meaning 'veil'. The veil or hood is a cloak of invisibility that was worn by several deities in order to conceal wisdom from the profane, and the hooded Silbury Hag is well within this tradition. The various folkloric Cailleachs were also known as the 'Great Old One', or the 'Mountain Mother' and the majority of these hags were cairn and mountain builders. The Hag at Silbury sits opposite Europe's tallest artificial mound!

The Cailleach Bhéara is a hag who is enshrined in Irish and Scottish folklore. She originated from the Bhéara Peninsula in Munster and her age is attested by a West Connacht proverb: 'Three great ages: the age of the yew tree, the age of the eagle, and the age of the Old Woman of Beare.'[21] The Cailleach Bhéara played an active role in farming and participated in mowing contests. She is said to have created several ancient monuments such as Newgrange by dropping stones from her apron as she strode across the land.[22] In Scotland she is known as the legendary creator of the Hebrides and the Isle of Mull, both also being formed by the loose rocks that fell from her apron. Slieve Gullion is a prominent mountain in South Armagh and on its summit near a lake is a Neolithic chambered cairn, known locally as The Cailleach Birrn's House or Cally Berry House.[23] Patterson recorded the following account from Creggan parish:

Often I started up the mountain to see the lake, but I could never tread the whole road, I was so afraid; for you know, a wedding party went into the Cally Berry house once and they were turned into stone. Her house goes down and down, and in the very bottom chamber sits the Cally herself, to this day, and will, maybe till the end of time.[24]

The farmer here is emphatic that the 'Cally' actually resides within the Neolithic chambered cairn and that she may even remain there for all eternity; an assertion that the Cailleach's power will never wane. Up until 1938 a stone was whitewashed religiously every year by locals for they believed that the Cailleach Bhéara had thrown it from Slieve Gullion.[25] It is evident that the Cailleach Bhéara was seen to be responsible for shaping the land in various regions and was connected with ancient ceremonial sites: indicating her sheer longevity as a mythological figure.

Other Irish hags were the Cailleach Bholais of the Inveragh Peninsula, the Cailleach Daingin of the Dingle Peninsula, the Cailleach Dhuibhneach and the Cailleach Laighneach from Munster and Leinster respectively.[26] The two latter mountain hags lived together in a cave called *Cro no Caillighe* (the Hag's Fold) and following a quarrel one of them killed the other by throwing her over a cliff.[27] The Cailleach Dhuibhneach was a local hag and the Cailleach Laighneach was an interloper, therefore it is possible that every region in Ireland and Britain had their own territorial mythological hag character as *genius loci*. In the Scottish Highlands there are legends of a hag known as the Cailleach Beinne Bric who could be encountered near a spring, or driving deer over the hills.[28] Numerous Celtic hags were associated with water or sacred wells and the hag at Silbury is clearly in this category: she is created by the nearby springs and the Winterbourne.

An important aspect concerning the Cailleach of the Scottish folklore is that she is known to have frequently been spotted driving animals over hills. A fascinating report of a three-day festival that occurred on the summit of Silbury Hill was published in the *Gloucester Journal* on 9th November 1736.[29] It records that a meal was served on the top of the hill and that approximately 5,000 people sat around Silbury. A bull was baited at the top and bottom of the hill and there was also bowling, backsword, wrestling and dancing. The same events took place on the second day, 'and also running round the hill for a petticoat. The 3rd day the bull was divided by Mr Smith amongst his poor neighbours on top of the hill where they diverted themselves with bonfires, ale, and roast beef, for several hours'.[30] John Goulstone, a researcher of the ritual origins of traditional games, wrote in *Antiquity* that this festival on Silbury's summit was an isolated event that had been organized by a landowner. He says:

Even so, certain seemingly traditional features of the games, like the race around the base of the hill – a local form of the customary virgins' smock race – give the impression that Silbury must have had a long association with this kind of rural festival. Indeed the perilous procedure of drawing a bull for baiting well over a hundred feet up a steep grassy slope, to a summit where in fact relatively few people could hope to obtain a proper view and where, one gathers, the beast was finally killed and roasted, tends to suggest a ritual activity of very early, perhaps pre-Christian, provenance.[31]

The Cailleach Beinne Bric was renowned for driving animals over the Scottish hills, and the Irish Cailleach Bhéara possessed a magical bull, so the Silbury Hag could have had similar legends attached to her. The three-day festival that involved a bull being driven up Silbury Hill could well have been the dying phase of an immemorial Samhain custom concerning the Silbury Hag, that had shed its obvious connections with paganism by the 1700s.

It is possible to adduce ancient Neolithic rites from the colourful farming traditions that are associated with the Hag. We have already witnessed the significance of the Maiden corn dolly and the Corn Baby, but if the harvest was late the dolly was called the Hag or Old Woman (Cailleach). In the Scottish Isle of Lewis the hag dolly was dressed up in clothes with an apron tied about her waist that was filled with cheese, bread and a sickle.[32] Here we notice a repetition of the apron motif that habitually featured in early folklore – the apron signifying guardianship and midwifery because the stones dropping from it are a euphemism for giving birth. The apron on the Cailleach dolly contained food and a sickle, and an old man from Ballymoyer recalled a sickle tradition involving this hag figure in 1944: 'I saw the Cailleach cut by the scythe only. It was afterwards taken into the house and put around the woman of the house.'[33] In Belfast the last sheaf was called the Granny and throughout Ulster the Cailleach was ceremonially cut after each farmer had thrown their sickle at her. In the south-east perimeter of Silbury Hill a perforated stone was discovered that had been used as a sickle-sharpener.[34] Could this sickle-sharpener have been a votive offering to the Silbury Winter Hag due to the sickle's significance in farming ceremonies, and the mythology pertaining to the Hag-deity?

The farmer that brought home the last load of grain in Ireland was called Winter. Dirty water was subsequently thrown over him and his face was blackened.[35] In Pembrokeshire in Wales, a similar tradition was maintained: a reaper carried the Cailleach dolly home and the other men drenched him with water as they tried to snatch the dolly from him.[36] If he managed to get home safe then he could keep the hag on his farm till the following spring. The farmer then mixed whatever grain remained intact on the dolly with the seed he intended to plant, or he fed it to his horse: 'both acts serving to insure fertility.'[37] The manner in which this material representation of the Hag was treated is a testimony to the enduring belief in the blessings she could bestow. A similar practice was observed in Poland, whereby the last sheaf was made into a dolly called *Baba* meaning Grandmother, and the woman who bound it would be drenched with water.

The Cailleach did not only appear in the farming community at the end of the harvest, but her presence was felt throughout the entire winter period. A character known as Mollie, Judy or Old Woman accompanied the Hodening Horse of the Hallowe'en and Midwinter festivities.[38] The Mollie was a man dressed as an old woman, who carried a broom which he used to sweep the doorstep of each house the horse visited. This ritual sweeping was a way to expell any ill-luck that may have befallen the household that year. In parts of Scotland a log was carved at Christmas time to resemble an old woman and was placed in the hearth to burn.[39] The log was called the *Cailleach Nollaich*, or Christmas Old Wife; the personification of winter and its dark, dismal nights. Its symbolic burning represented the farmers' desires for the coming new year to be prosperous, and for the Hag to become the Spring

Maiden; the new triumphing over the old, warmth abating cold.

Alexander Carmichael noted a custom that was practised by the island dwellers of Scotland on New Year's Eve or 'Hogmanay' (known as 'hagmena' in previous centuries). A group of men called the *gillean Callaig* carollers travelled about the village at night, along with a man who was dressed in a bull's hide that had the horns and hoofs still attached to it:

'When the men come to a house they ascend the wall and run round sunwise, the man in the hide shaking the horns and hoofs, and the other men striking the hard hide with sticks. The appearance of the man in the hide is gruesome, while the din is terrific. Having descended and recited their runes at the door, the Hogmanay men are admitted and treated to the best in the house.'[40]

The opening lines of the *Cairioll Callaig* (Hogmanay Carol) attest the age of the custom:

> I am now come to your country,
> To renew to you the Hogmanay
> I need not tell you of it,
> It was in the time of our forefathers.[41]

This is the remnant of an archaic rite that was initially centred around the partnership between the Hag and the Bull. The Winter Hag was the Goddess Of Death and Regeneration who possessed the keys to the gates of the New Year; the Bull was associated with death, renewal and the Otherworld and it cracked open the 'Egg of the Year' with its horns. The Egyptian *Book of the Dead* outlines a rite involving the deceased being wrapped in a bull's hide, and the Bards of Britain and Ireland would undergo an incubatory sleep wrapped in a bull's skin in order to receive messages from the Otherworld.[42] The man dressed in the bull's hide on the Eve of a New Year embodied all the elements associated with that period. The Christmas Bull was also a popular custom in Wiltshire, Dorset and Gloucestershire. A man wearing a hollowed out bull's head was accompanied by a keeper and a band of men and boys who would visit the houses in the village.[43] He travelled at dusk and nobody knew when he might appear:

'He was given the freedom of every house and allowed to penetrate into any room, escorted by his keeper. The whole company would flee before his formidable horns, the more so as, towards the end of the evening, neither the Bull nor his keeper could be certified as strictly sober.'[44] In Tetbury in Gloucestershire a wooden bull's head with long horns, white face and black staring eyes was carried from door-to-door covered with sacking. When each door was opened the bull was unveiled and displayed to the householder. The Gloucestershire head had belonged to the same family for four generations, and at Stourton in Wiltshire a Christmas Bull had remained in a family for over a century.[45]

The Hag was also associated with Christmas time in Teutonic lore. Brechta,

Bertha, Berchte or Perchta was a small old woman believed to dwell in a hollow mountain, and to watch over agriculture. She was a pre-christian midwinter goddess who later became associated with the Epiphany, the eve of Twelfth Night, as the Epiphany was known as *Berchtentag*, or Berchte's day.[46] Berchte was concerned with the tidiness of barns, and as the special patroness of spinning she was known to peer through the window of every house between Christmas and January 6th to inspect that household's spinning. Similarly, in rural Ireland, it was said that a hag would enter houses where spinning was taking place late at night and would help with the work. During the Christmas period Berchte rewarded all diligent women with a present of one of her own golden threads, or a distaff full of fine flax; 'but wherever a careless spinner was found, her wheel was broken, her flax soiled, and if she had failed to honour the goddess by eating plenty of the cakes baked at that period of the year, she was cruelly punished.'[47] This would seem to be the genesis of the Santa Claus story for we see the Winter Hag rewarding those that have been conscientious, and one of her alternative names was *Butzenbercht*, meaning 'the bringer of gifts'.[48]

The Hag was also said to be the leader of the Wild Hunt and to have a howling host of wild animals that followed her at night-time; Santa also travelled at night with his team of reindeer. In various Alpine areas it was customary for the villagers to put food on the roof for Berchte on the eve of the Epiphany, in other places they would eat pancakes or dumplings and leave the remainder on the table for her. Children nowadays leave food out for Santa on Christmas Eve. Berchte was said to be very fond of children and sometimes she was seen travelling with a large group of them, or she would enter into a room where a baby was left alone and rock its cradle. Berchte is still used as a threat to lazy or naughty youngsters in various regions of southern Germany, Switzerland, Alsace and Austria.[49]

Befana the old woman of midwinter who features in Italian folklore is very similar to Berchte. Befana would leave presents for sleeping children in the stockings they hung up for her, and she was also associated with the Epiphany. The word itself could be a corruption of her name, for Epiphany is from the Greek *ephiphaneia* meaning 'apparition', and the pre-christian Befana or Befania was known to appear in ghost form around the winter solstice. Doll effigies of Befana were displayed in the windows and a tremendous noise was made in her honour with tambourines, trumpets, tin horns and drums. This is similar to the Christmas Bull tradition in Wiltshire whereby the people accompanying the Bull made a very loud noise.

Befana was taken over by Christian hagiography for she later appears as St Befana. In Christian legend St Befana was invited by the Magi to accompany them as they travelled to see the infant Jesus, 'but she said she was too busy cleaning her house. Later she attempted to follow, but became lost and never saw the Holy Child. Every year she comes looking for him.'[50]

There is a strong possibility that this legend is distorted and that Befana's true role concerning the birth of Jesus was disguised. A Latin Infancy Gospel from the Christian Apocrypha describes how a midwife heard that a woman (Mary) was about to give birth to her first child in a cave.[51] The midwife sent a girl on ahead of her with a birthing chair and when the midwife arrived she asked Joseph 'Who is the young woman who will give birth in this cave?'[52] Joseph explained that Mary was not yet his wife and that she was 'made pregnant by the Holy Spirit'. The midwife watched over Mary during the delivery and then declared that she was indeed a virgin who had inexplicably given birth. Most midwives in the past were old women who were experienced in parturition and had a knowledge of herbs. The birthing chair was the throne of the Triple Goddess, the Hag in particular, and the enthroned Goddess was a popular motif in ancient art. The midwife in the Latin Gospel could well have been the Italian goddess Befana, which would explain why she was particularly associated with the Epiphany. In this Gospel from the Christian Apocrypha (In Greek *apokryphos* means 'things hidden') it was the Hag as midwife who confirmed that the Christ Child was born of a virgin. The details of the original legend were more likely to have been that Befana was midwife to Mary and that she had informed the Magi as to the nature of the miraculous birth, and not that she had stayed at home cleaning instead.

The Hag was a predominant religious figure for thousands of years, and her worship was so widespread that she was adopted and adapted by the Christian Church, just as Ann and Bride were. The most interesting aspect of the Hag's assimilation is that of the female exhibitionist carvings found over the doorways, windows, or on the corbels of churches in Britain and Ireland that are known as *Sheela-na-Gigs*. Dating from the eleventh century onwards these conspicuous carvings are depictions of gaunt, naked females who are displaying their vulvas in a frank manner. Jack Roberts says that the term 'Sheela-na-Gig' is the anglicised form of the Irish *Síle na gCioch*, *Síle* meaning hag, or Spiritual Woman; *gCioch* or *Gíob* signifies breasts or buttocks, but it could also be linked to the word *Guí* which means to pray.[53] In 1936, Edith Guest recorded a meeting with a woman from the Macroom district in Ireland 'who understood the word sheela-na-gig as being an old woman of the type known commonly as a "hag".'[54] What do these hag figures represent, and why were they carved into many of our churches?

Some scholars believe that Sheela-na-gigs were part of the Christian Church's campaign against lust and immorality. Whilst some carvings depicting male and female figures engaged in the sexual act are obvious puritanical portrayals of the dangers of lust, there is overwhelming evidence that Sheela-na-gigs do not convey the same message; they are vestigial idols of the pagan religion, like the foliate Green Man. Sheelas are apotropaic figures that were believed to bring fertility and good luck due to their ability to avert the maleficent eye. Jack Roberts says: 'Johann Kohl, a German traveller to Ireland in the 1840s, recorded that the figures of displayed women on churches had something to do with the ancient custom of averting ill luck.'[55] It was considered lucky to rub the genitals of various Sheelas and the resulting dust from this action was thought to have healing powers – the Buckland Sheela in Buckinghamshire appears to bear marks of such rubbing.

Sheela-na-gigs were also carved onto Irish castles to ward off any attackers. In the early saga *Táin Bó Cúailnge* there is reference to women subduing the enemy by exposing their genitals.[56] Jørgen Anderson described the account of a traveller to Ireland in the nineteenth century who recorded the belief that a man who was afflicted with bad luck could ward off the curse if a prostitute exposed her genitals to him.[57] A letter to the *Irish Times* in 1977 from Walter Mahon-Smith demonstrates a further aspect of this practice that was still extant in the early 1900s:

In a townland near where I lived, a deadly feud had continued for generations between the families of two small farmers. One day, before the first World War, when the men of one of the families, armed with pitchforks and heavy blackthorn sticks, attacked the house of their enemy, the woman-of-the-house came to the door of her cottage, and in full sight of all (including my father and myself, who happened to be passing by) lifted her skirt and underclothes high above her head, displaying her naked genitals. The enemy of her and her family fled in terror.[58]

This feud was undoubtedly a land dispute, and the woman displayed herself to demonstrate her family's rightful sovereignty, thus thwarting the other party's claim and reflecting their malicious intentions back onto them with her actions, hence why they fled.

The Sheela-na-gigs on secular buildings fulfilled a tutelary role, and were perhaps localised portrayals of the territorial Divine Hag who bestowed sovereignty. In this manner, the Sheela that was associated with a castle not only protected the clan, but sanctified their right to the land, for without the Hag's patronage there can be no sovereignty. A Sheela carved on a key-stone at Ballinderry Castle is surrounded by a marigold, the emblem of long life; a triskele, a symbol of good fortune; a rose, emblem of fertility and resurrection, and a triquetra, an apotropaic symbol. The images that surround the Ballinderry Sheela were obviously intended to augment her powers.

In the medieval era, the coronation of the Pope involved the bizarre ceremonial act of sitting upon a porphyry birthing stool that was his throne. The reason given for this procedure was that an English woman called Joan had entered the priesthood disguised as a man, and rose to the position of Pope John VIII. Her secret was not discovered until she died in childbirth, and to prevent a woman ever entering the priesthood again the birthing stool was used so that the genitals of the Pope could be inspected whilst he sat on the chair naked underneath his gown. There is no evidence to prove the legend of Pope Joan, yet the practice was upheld for over five hundred years. The throne is now kept in a locked room in the Vatican Museum.

It is highly unlikely that the most important man in the medieval religious world would have subjected himself to such an embarrassing and degrading practice during his finest hour, so there had to be a symbolic significance to the birthing stool throne. Perhaps the act of sitting on a birthing stool was a tradition that was at the very foundations of the Catholic Church – similar to the coronation stone, the Stone of Scone – and that it was integral to receiving the Triple Crown. Porphyry is a semi-precious stone quarried in Egypt that was associated with 'Empire', and the Great Pharaohs of Egypt wore a triple crown to demonstrate the uniting of Upper, Middle and Lower Egypt. Neumann says that Isis (the Egyptian goddess) means 'the Seat or the Throne, the symbols of which she bears on her head.'[59] It is generally known that Wisdom is a Crown of Beauty, and the *Book of Sirach* or *Ecclesiasticus* meaning 'church book' (from the Old Testament Apocrypha) states: 'She will place upon him an eternal crown, and victory for all eternities among the saints.' Perhaps the elements of the Pope's coronation were inherited from paganism, involving the sovereignty of the future Pope being confirmed and blessed by the crowning aspect of the Trinity – the Hag of Wisdom, midwife to the Virgin Mary.

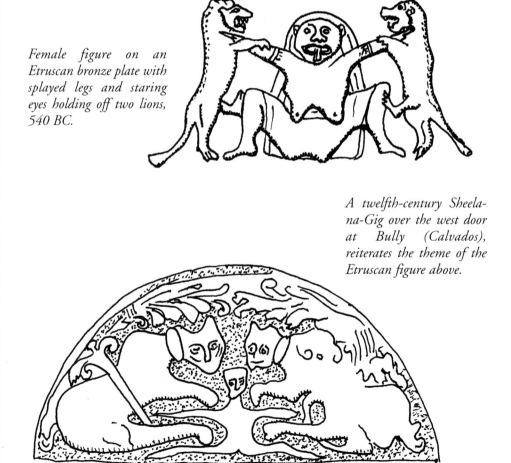

Female figure on an Etruscan bronze plate with splayed legs and staring eyes holding off two lions, 540 BC.

A twelfth-century Sheela-na-Gig over the west door at Bully (Calvados), reiterates the theme of the Etruscan figure above.

As we already know the Church absorbed many aspects from the pagan religion and many goddesses served Christianity as saints. A Sheela over the church doorway at Killinaboy is said to be an image of St Buidhe, and a figure at Ballyvourney in Munster is believed to be St Gobnait, otherwise known as the goddess Brigid.[60] The former owner of an old mill at Rosnaree recalls that the Sheela-na-gig there was 'the image of an original Goddess'.[61] Several goddesses appear in early mythology who have the same attributes as the later Sheelas, the Greek goddess Baubo being one example. Baubo was a hag who displayed her vulva to the grieving goddess Demeter. The gesture was a protective charm to avert the powers of death. There are several figures in ancient art that are clearly the iconographic predecessors to the medieval Sheela-na-gigs. Weir and Jerman noticed the similarities between a naked splay-legged female on an Etruscan bronze plate from 540 BC who is holding two flanking lions, and a twelfth-century Sheela-na-gig with splayed legs who is gripping two beasts.[62] A Viking picture stone from Gotland, Sweden, depicts a naked female holding two serpents. The snakes that are above her form a triple knot: a spell to ward off negative influences.[63] The medieval Sheela on the windowsill of Rath Blathmaic, Ireland, is a similar image.[64]

(Above) The female on a viking slab at Gotland, Sweden (400 BC) is similar to the medieval Sheela-na-gig on an Irish round tower (below).

On the end of a gold bracelet discovered in Reinheim (Saarland), dating from 400 BC is an exhibitionist 'owl-goddess'.[65] The owl was associated with wisdom and it was also considered to be an earthly incarnation of the Hag Goddess. In Scottish Gaelic the owl is called the *cailleach oidhche*, the 'night hag'.[66]

An oak figurine that was retrieved from a peat bog in Ballachulish, Scotland, dating approximately from the seventh century BC was discovered with traces of wickerwork, suggesting that she was housed in a wicker shrine; Anne Ross noticed that she appears to be an image of the Cailleach. This Celtic carving reflects the legends of the Cally residing in her 'house', such as the Neolithic chambered cairn on Slieve Gullion. Cheryl Straffon describes a custom surrounding the Cailleach and her house that is associated with a place called *Glen Cailliche* in Scotland. Every year at Beltane a shepherd would take some stones from inside a small stone 'house' and set them up near a burn called *Allt Cailliche* (the Hag's Stream):

'These stones which came from the river nearby, were known as the Cailliche and her family, and their function was to watch over the glen and the well-being of the cattle. Then every year at the Celtic festival of Samhain (at the beginning of November) the stones would be replaced in the small stone house made for them. The house was formerly thatched, and it was part of the ritual to re-thatch it every year.'[67] The house is called *Tigh nam Cailliche*, the Hag's House.[68] The Ballachulish figurine found with traces of her 'house' has hag-like features and her hands point to her vulva, which is one of the characteristics of the later Sheela-na-gigs.

Oak figurine retrieved from a peat bog in Ballachulish, Scotland, dating from 700 BC.

The Destruction of Da Derga's Hostel is part of what is known as the 'Mythological Cycle' of the Irish tales. There is a hag in the tale who displays many of the physical aspects of the medieval Sheelas: 'a woman, big-mouthed, huge, dark, ugly, hideous, was behind him. Though her snout were flung on a branch, the branch would support it. Her pudenda reached to her knees.'[69] In the church at Oaksey, Wiltshire, there is a remarkable Sheela-na-gig whose vast vulva hangs down to her knees.

Sheela-na-gig in the church at Oaksey, Wiltshire, that mirrors the Hag of ancient Irish tales who has a vulva reaching to her knees.

In the church at Winterbourne Monkton, only two miles north of Silbury, there is a carving of a naked hooded female on the twelfth-century font who is displaying her vulva from which vegetation sprouts. She is surrounded by zig-zags or chevrons, the ancient symbol for water, and here it is clearly a depiction of the Winterbourne. In her raised right arm she holds a sickle; could this hooded figure be a representation of the Silbury Hag? She holds the very farming implement that was associated with the Hag, and a sickle-sharpener was discovered at Silbury. The water that surrounds her is the Winterbourne that in conjuction with the nearby springs creates the Silbury Water Meadow Hag, and the fact that she is a Sheela-na-gig means she is a carving of the Hag aspect!

It is obvious that the Sheela-na-gigs were symbolic representations of the Holy Hag and that they were believed to have magical powers. In Wiltshire, old carters would put stones that had a natural hole through them on a string, and hang them in the stable to protect their horses from illness and spells. These stones were known as 'hag stones', offering similar beneficent qualities to the Sheela-na-gigs.

During the Reformation many Sheelas were unfortunately defaced, completely destroyed, or hidden. In Irish folklore there are tales of the Hag coming into direct conflict with the Church. One legend explains how an old woman triumphs over Saint Moling at Mullinakill, causing him to leave the district.[70] In another tale a hag does not allow Saint Patrick to erect a church near Ardagh Hill:
'One morning early when he was building it a small red-haired woman appeared and spoke something to him. St Patrick gave a hop, stop and jump on one of the stones and fled.'[71] In Teevurcher, however, Saint Patrick overcame the Cailleach Ghearagain of that district, and then struck her into four pieces with his staff. A piece of her body landed in the lake, and it is said that one day she will rise again.[72] The Cailleach Bhéara was Christianized and became a veiled nun, blessed by Cummine of the monastery of Clonfert. These stories indicate that in some areas the veneration of the Divine Hag was accepted by the Church and she was allowed to remain dominant, whilst in others she was not tolerated at all. This led to the inevitable demonization of the hag figure as the wicked, warty witch that sucks children's blood disguised as a screech-owl, and terrorizes people at Hallowe'en. The prehistoric Hag could never really be eradicated: memories of her live on in farming customs, children's fairy tales such as *Hansel and Gretel* and in language. The word for a dish comprised of organ meats for example is haggis which means 'hag's dish'. Although it is the traditional Scottish dish it was also eaten in England up until the eighteenth century, and like the word haggard, that means 'wild-looking', it is a recollection of the once powerful Old Hag, for language is 'fossil poetry'.

There is substantive evidence that the Hag was an eminent figure throughout the ages so with this knowledge it does appear that the Silbury Hag was an architectural icon. It is impossible to precisely determine who her designers were without extensive excavation and dating of the site, but there are several factors that indicate she could possibly date back to the Neolithic era. The 'hooded flint hag' retrieved from West Kennet long barrow that is so remarkably similar to the Silbury Hag is certainly enticing; the egg-shaped pools and her striking appearance only in the winter period are links with prehistoric art and mythology. The most telling aspect however is the sheer poetic message she conveys alongside that most mysterious Neolithic legacy – Silbury Hill. Prehistoric peoples had a mythopoeic perception, this is reinforced by the fact that Neolithic artists chose the Avebury area as such a vast canvas for their religious architectural forms. The Silbury Hag oversees the Silbury Mother Goddess whilst casting an eye to her next transformation – Swallowhead spring the maidenhead.

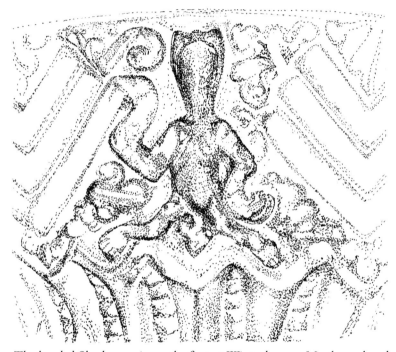

The hooded Sheela-na-gig on the font at Winterbourne Monkton church, two miles north of Silbury Hill. She holds a sickle, the implement associated with the Hag.

In 1993, a Romano-British settlement consisting of five separate stone built buildings was discovered on the flat ground of the Winterbourne valley, that had been blanketed by over one metre of hillwash and alluvium.[73] Romano-British buildings that are stone built are 'rarely encountered in the Avebury area or, for that matter elsewhere in Wessex' which denotes that the settlement was of considerable importance.[74] The site was built to the east of the Silbury Hag, on the opposite side of the Winterbourne. The Romans took a religious interest in the prehistoric monuments of the Silbury complex. Professor Piggott discovered six Roman coins in the forecourt of West Kennet long barrow that he believed were votive offerings, and not 'casual losses'.[75] There are several wells near Silbury and the Swallowhead that have been attributed to the Romans because they contained Roman coins and pottery. However, these wells could have been what are known as 'ritual shafts', other examples of which do exist in Britain that date back to the second millennium BC. Kenneth Watts says:

'It is possible that here the Romans converted existing prehistoric ritual shafts into wells for their travellers, or they may have continued to use them as they too made use of votive offering shafts which often contain a great variety of gifts to the deity. These have been confused with wells because their tops were often constructed of vaulted masonry.'[76] The shafts or wells provided a ceremonial focal point for worship of the springs and the sacred Kennet.

A fascinating point concerning the bridge that crosses the Winterbourne is that it is called Pan Bridge. Pan was a Greek pastoral deity who protected flocks and herds, and who loved hills and lonely places. His name is derived from the root *pa*, found in the Latin *pasco* or *panis*, meaning 'the Feeder, the herdsman'.[77] Pan was half-human and had the horns, ears, legs and beard of a goat. He was renowned for his amorous antics: virility being the necessary attribute of a god that was a denizen of wild nature. He enjoyed travelling across pastures and through woods, and at noon he rested near streams. In Classical art he was often depicted dancing and playing the musical instrument that he invented – the panpipes. His original panpipes were kept at Ephesus in the cave of the goddess Diana.[78]

Pan was native to Arcadia but his cult spread throughout Greece, and he was assimilated into the Roman culture. The existence of a large Roman site that skirts the hag would seem to indicate that it was the Romans who introduced Pan into the Silbury mythological arena. The Romans built a road running between Mildenhall (Cunetio) and Bath (Aquae Sulis) that respectfully steered around Silbury Hill. It was this road, and the existence of the settlement so close to it, that will have necessitated the building of a bridge across the Winterbourne. The Romans then dedicating the bridge to the god Pan. A stone decorated with the image of a naked horned god was actually built into a Roman bridge in Cumberland, suggesting perhaps that Pan, and other male horned deities, had an association with bridges.[79] Records show that in 1823 Pan bridge was dilapidated by a major flood and had to be rebuilt, and in 1932 it was rebuilt yet again. This clearly indicates that the seasonal flooding of the Winterbourne has constantly damaged the bridge there, and explains why nothing structural remains of the original Roman bridge; the associated name, however, could not be washed away.

At Silbury we have all aspects of the Trinity and the inclusion of a male god who mirrors the prehistoric portrayals of an animalistic consort. From the seventh millennium onwards, representations of a he-goat deity appeared in European sculptural art. Several male figurines were depicted with goat masks, and images of a goat god also appeared on ritual vessels.[80] Pan bridge is adjacent to the egg-shaped pools and lies half way between Swallowhead springs and the Silbury Hag. Its positioning could be symbolic of the consort/king mating with the Hag-Maiden. In Irish mythology the battle-goddess the Morrigán had sexual intercourse with the Dagdha over a stream.[81] Pan the protector of flocks mated with the Water Meadow Hag that gave the sheep lush pasture, and thereupon the Hag transformed into the Cunnit maiden.

The goat god Pan, the protector of the flocks.

Pipe a song about a Lamb (*William Blake*)

Pan was the god of shepherds and the flocks and in the sixteenth century it was said that Christ was 'the verye Pan and god of Shepheards.'[82] John the Baptist could equally be equated with Pan for he was the voice that cried in the wilderness, just as

Pan was said to do. The Baptist survived on a diet of locusts and wild honey and emerged from the wilderness dressed in a raiment of camel hair and a loincloth of leather. John's apparel was that of the classic wild man and he was often depicted holding a lamb in his right hand.

The Church did not eradicate paganism: in order to gain acceptance among the peasantry it payed due obeisance to the seasonal dictates of the pre-Christian calendar, although the festivals themselves were coated with a veneer of Christianity. Goddesses were canonized, pagan motifs such as Sheela-na-gigs and Green Men were adopted, and the essence of Pan's identity was Christianized. The Church did eventually endeavour to dissuade the farming community from having any association with paganism, and so the horned and cloven-hoofed elements from Pan's image were incorporated into the medieval Church's artistic impressions of the Devil. It was hoped that the Devil's image and association with a specific place would instill superstitious fear, and deter the countryfolk from pagan ways. Many old bridges in England are called 'Devil's bridge', perhaps they had originally been associated with Pan, or a similar pagan horned god.

There is a folktale that Silbury Hill was created by the Devil. The original words of the story had been retained by a family in Melksham for over three hundred years and were published in *Folk-Lore* in 1913:

When Stonehenge was built, a goodish bit after Avebury, the Devil were in a rare taking. 'There's getting a vast deal too much religion in these here parts,' he says, 'summat must be done.' So he picks up his shovel, and cuts a slice out of Salisbury plain, and sets off for to smother up Avebury. But the priests saw him coming and set to work with their charms and incussations, and they fixed him while he wer yet a nice way off, till at last he flings down his shovelful just where he stood. And *that's* Silbury.[83]

The uneducated local somehow knew that Avebury predates Stonehenge, but the intriguing aspect of the tale is that the Devil enters into battle with priests from Avebury who use magical charms to defeat him. In another version of the tale the Devil is thwarted by Saint John who just happens to be in the area.[84]

The Alton Goddess similarly became associated with the Devil for the serpentine umbilical cord on Knap Hill became the Devil's Trackway. The highest peak of Tan Hill was marked on an old map as the Devil's Church. A standing stone that previously stood below Milk Hill was noted on the Pembroke Estate map of 1784 as the Devil's Church Stone, and a stretch of arable land nearby was called the Devil's Church Furlong. Despite pressure from the Church the Wiltshire countryfolk maintained the old traditions, which ensured the preservation of old names such as Cunnit and Pan Bridge. Aubrey Burl informs us that: 'the Wiltshire peasantry, superstitious and conservative, continued in the ways of their forefathers ignoring the cajoling of Christian preachers with their foreign notions.'[85]

The names, traditions and beliefs that have survived from the distant past reveal the presence, identity and mythological role of the embedded deities of the Silbury complex: and from these clues, and the archæological evidence, we can begin to interpret Silbury's significance in the surrounding ritual landscape.

CHAPTER SIX

THE MYSTERIES OF AVEBURY

May these stones of song
Ever brighten the treasury of Britain

From the *Death Song of Uther Pendragon*
(trans. John Matthews)[1]

The Avebury region is one of the best survivals of a Neolithic landscape, the sheer size and complexity of the monuments attest that the area was of prime importance to the Neolithic communities. Windmill Hill, the 'grandmother of Avebury's sacred landscape'[2] was used by the Neolithic farmers from 3700 BC onwards. The causewayed enclosure that was built there around 3400 BC was a seasonal gathering place for rituals, this is borne out by the discovery of several carved chalk phalli, chalk balls, miniature 'cups' and roughly-shaped goddess figurines. The presence of stone axes, and pottery from different parts of the country, suggests it was also the centre for trade.

The construction of West Kennet long barrow began around 3700 BC, and excavations have revealed that it was the site of collective burial, and elaborate rituals concerning death and rebirth. The ancient monument called the Sanctuary that previously stood on Overton Hill was first constructed around 3000 BC, and during the earliest phases of its use it seems to have been linked to West Kennet long barrow. It originally consisted of a circular, wooden building with a thatched roof that was gradually extended over the centuries. An abundance of human bones were discovered at the site which, along with the presence of burnt bones in the chambers of West Kennet long barrow, indicates that it was most likely a mortuary house where the corpses were defleshed by excarnation, so that the clean bones could then be deposited in the long barrow. A lump of haematite was found at the Sanctuary which would have been used in rites of the dead. Several skulls seem to have been removed from the barrow and taken to Windmill Hill, which evokes the image of ceremonial processions to and from these early monuments, and highlights their interconnectedness.

The principal function of West Kennet long barrow was to provide a womb from which the dead ancestors could be reborn. In prehistoric mythology the Mother Goddess that gave birth to all life became the Hag Goddess who presided over the dead. We have seen that a piece of limestone which astonishingly resembles a hag was ritually placed on the roof of the chambered area in a long barrow at Notgrove, Gloucestershire; this limestone hag was obviously the protectress of the dead interred within the barrow, which explains why she was placed in an overseeing position, on the roof. The passage grave at Slieve Gullion in Ireland, was believed to be the residence of the powerful Cailleach Bhéara, who, according to local tradition would reside in this 'house' for ever. Sheela-na-gigs are images of the Hag Goddess that were carved on churches and secular buildings to fulfill a tutelary role. A votive flint offering that resembles a hooded hag (perhaps even the Silbury Water Meadow Hag) was placed within the west chamber of West Kennet long barrow in order to watch over the dead. The long barrow was a subtle combination of the key aspects of the Triple Goddess, and given that it was a ritual centre for the living for roughly a thousand years this is not surprising.

Around the time that Silbury Hill was in use, West Kennet long barrow fell into disuse. The chambers and the passage of the barrow were completely filled in with chalk rubble, and the entrance was then sealed off with huge sarsen boulders. The Neolithic religion had obviously advanced to a higher stage upon completion of the Silbury temple.

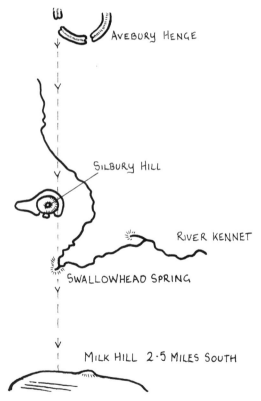

The sculptural monument of Silbury Hill was built to represent the Earth Mother; the hill was her gigantic pregnant belly and the surrounding water-filled moat defined her body. The only finds retrieved from excavations of the mound were votive offerings such as antlers and mistletoe. Roman historians recorded that mistletoe was sacred to the Celtic Druids: it was the emblem that symbolized the crown of their mysteries because its shape was synonymous with the orb of the sun, and its leaves resembled wings. Its glutinous white berries were seen as the semen of the Sun God and mistletoe was thus associated with fertility. The mistletoe offerings were placed inside the hill (the womb) by the Neolithic farmers as a sacred act of mystical impregnation of the Silbury Goddess by the sun, so

North-south axis line that runs from Avebury Henge through Silbury Hill, Swallowhead spring and on to Milk Hill.

that she, like the Alton Goddess, would then give birth to the harvest at Lughnasadh.

Michael Dames observed that Silbury Hill was built on an axis line that runs from the west entrance of Avebury Henge to Milk Hill, and that 'all full moons and all mid-day suns reach highest altitude on this line.'[3] The axis line connects the monumental forms of the Avebury Serpent Temple, the Silbury Mother Goddess and the Alton Mother Goddess. Silbury Hill is also aligned with the midwinter and midsummer solstice sunrise so it was undoubtedly the central focus for seasonal rituals in the area.

West Kennet long barrow had once incorporated all the elements of the Triple Goddess within one monument, but now the concept was represented separately in the landscape. The maiden Cunnit waters defined the image of the Great Mother Silbury, and the Winterbourne created the gigantic Water Meadow Hag, although it is impossible to state for certain where the Silbury Hag appeared in the chronological order of the construction of monuments. The majority of Celtic hags were mythological cairn and mountain builders, or were referred to as sitting on or next to mountains, and the Silbury Hag sits opposite Europe's tallest artificial mound.

The climax of the Avebury ceremonial landscape was the construction of the henge, stone circles and stone avenues that created a vast temple precinct across several miles of the countryside. The Avebury megalithic complex was a religious and cultural centre that attracted people from many other regions. Its close proximity to the Ridgeway/Icknield Way ensured that links were established with areas such as Somerset, Cornwall, East Anglia and possibly Grimes Graves flint mines in Norfolk. The discovery of stone axes from Wales, and pottery made from gabbroic clay unique to the Lizard Head in Cornwall provide evidence of long-distance trade. Avebury was a vast metropolis, and as R. Hippisley Cox says there is a strong possibility that it was the hub of the country.[4] Furthermore, seventy seven Egyptian faience beads dating from approximately 1600 BC were discovered in twenty three Wiltshire barrows, including a barrow on Tan Hill, and this is eight more than have been found in the rest of Great Britain and western Europe,[5] highlighting that Wiltshire's magnetism extended far beyond the British Isles.

William Stukeley was a clergyman and a Freemason and he understood the philosophy and mysteries of the hermetic arts. Based on his studies of comparative religion he concluded:
'The plan on which Abury was built, is that sacred hierogram of the Egyptians and other ancient nations, the circle and the snake. The whole figure is the circle, snake and wings.'

Avebury was a spectacular 'winged temple', the ancient symbol of alchemical fusion laid out large in the landscape. The Neolithic henge and stone circles of Avebury created the Holy Circle, signifying Nature's cycle of infinitude like the ancient alchemical figure the ouroboros – a serpent coiled in a circle that is biting its own tail. The two sinuous avenues were added to the henge and stone circles during the Beaker period (around 2500 BC to 1800 BC), and circles of stones were built around the Sanctuary site also at this time. The West Kennet Avenue connected the Avebury Henge with the Sanctuary over a mile away, and it appears to have been a processional route between both monuments. The avenues created the image of a gigantic stone serpent, and the stones around the Sanctuary accentuated the snake's head. If the serpent's head is severed at *Hack*pen Hill ('pen' being an old word for head) following the true dragon-slaying tradition, the Avebury Serpent is then the alate circle proper. The *anima mundi*, or Cneph (the Divine Spirit) is released as a consequence: a practice which was known to the alchemists as The Great Work.

Stukeley envisaged the entire Avebury complex as the Divine Marriage set in stone. The avenue serpent represented eternity, the outer stone circle was the earth, and the two inner circles were the sun and moon. These elements represented the fusion of the opposites – day and night, light and dark, fire and water, male and female. The serpent with its multivalent symbolism was the embodiment of dualism – it was intimately connected with the Goddess, but it was also associated with the male aspect due to its long, muscular shape being suggestive of the phallus. Within the centre of the solar South Circle was the 21 feet (6.3 m) high Obelisk, the *axis mundi* around which the world revolved. The South Circle is aligned to the Beltane sunrise and what is interesting is that well into the nineteenth century villagers used to dance around a maypole that stood in the South Circle, 'perhaps unconsciously echoing dances and rituals performed there thousands of years before.'[6] The Cove inside the lunar North Circle represented the feminine principle; it is aligned to the midsummer sunrise and faces towards the most northerly rising of the moon.[7]

The sinuous path of the West Kennet Avenue, and the confirmation of the previous existence of both the Beckhampton Avenue and the Sanctuary, attest the relative accuracy of Stukeley's groundplan. This, coupled with the folktale of serpents being unable to live in Avebury's stone circles, and the carving of a bishop killing a dragon/serpent in the village church adds weight to Stukeley's theory. The snake was associated with water due to its meandering movements, its powers of renewal and its supposed ability to procure rain; the West Kennet Avenue originally ran close to the Kennet river that disappeared in the summer, and magically re-appeared at Óimelc, the period when snakes return from hibernation. The Downs around Avebury are also the meeting-place of the three main watersheds of England.[8] The circle, snake and wings, or flying orb, that can be seen at Avebury were all attributes of the god Cneph, or Ptah (the architect of the gods), and John Michell says that wherever Cneph was invoked 'he was replaced by St Catherine and her wheel.'[9] St Catherine was a dragon-slaying saint and was often portrayed in Renaissance art with an S-shaped posture to indicate her association with the secret of the Serpent. What is fascinating is that the public house where Stukeley and other antiquarians stayed in Avebury was called 'The Catherine Wheel Inn'.

Alexander Keiller, the founder of the Morven Institute of Archæological Research, began excavating the West Kennet Avenue in 1934. Several of the avenue stones had fallen or had been buried, so Keiller and Piggott supervised its restoration. During the re-erection of the stones they discovered two carvings on stone 25S which they classified as 'cup and ring' markings.

Two carvings on stone 25S, The West Kennet Avenue. The uppermost carving is a cup and ring and the lower carving is an ouroboros, the ancient symbol of infinity.

Piggott noted that the carvings 'show irregular double concentric circles surrounding a pair of depressions, of which in each instance one is a natural hole in the sarsen and the other is artificially worked.'[10] The stone was put back in place but now only the upper carving is fully visible, most of the lower carving is below ground. The topmost carving is centred around a natural hole, but the carving that is partially submerged astonishingly resembles an ouroboros. In the winter when the rest of the serpent population is in hibernation, the carving on stone 25S emerges from the Underworld: this is because the grass around the base of the stone is closely grazed at that time of year. In these conditions the carving can actually be inspected first hand, where it is easy to identify that the head and eye of the ouroboros have, in fact, been artificially pecked out just as Piggott stated. When Keiller and Piggott examined the stone they mis-classified the carving as a 'cup and ring' and because it now lies underground it has been forgotten.

The ouroboros is the emblem of perfection, omniscience and immortality because it consumes itself to itself. This carving substantiates Stukeley's theory that Avebury is a winged Serpent Temple, because it appears to depict the chimeric fusion of a bird's head and tail with a serpent's body. The ouroboros on stone 25S is beaked, and the tail artistically implies the plumage of a swan's tail, delivering the overall impression of a serpent with the ability to fly – the winged serpent and circle (Cneph).

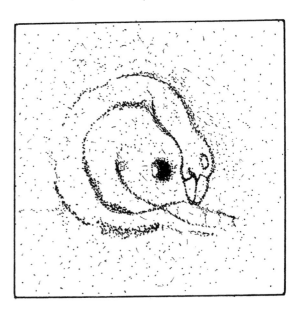

Detailed sketch of the ouroboros carving on stone 25S at Avebury.

The entire Avebury complex is similar to a gigantic winged serpent and it stretches around Silbury Hill, an aspect that Sir R.C. Hoare commented upon: 'Two avenues, like wings, expand themselves to the right and left, as if to protect the hallowed sanctuary and holy mount.'[11] Stukeley also says:

Silbury stands exactly south of Abury, and exactly between the extremities of the two avenues, the head and tail of the snake. The work of Abury, which is the circle, and the two avenues which represent the snake transmitted through it, are the hierogrammaton, or sacred prophylactic character of the Divine Mind, which is to protect the depositum of the prince here interred. The Egyptians, for the very same reason, frequently pictured the same hieroglyphic upon the breast of their mummies; and very frequently on the top and summit of Egyptian obelisks, this picture of the serpent and circle is seen, and upon an infinity of their monuments. In the very same manner, this huge snake and circle, made of stones, hangs as it were brooding over Silbury Hill, in order to bring again to a new life the person buried there.[12]

In Stukeley's era it was the general consensus that Silbury was the grave of a chieftain or king, and it was only the thorough archæological and scientific surveys of the 1967 excavation that finally laid the King Sil theory to rest. In the mythologised landscape, the Avebury megalithic complex could more appropriately be viewed as the giant serpent or dragon who was always the guardian of treasure in ancient mythology. There is a legend that King Sil's treasure is hidden within Silbury Hill but the treasure is not the statue of a golden rider, it is occult gold: the hidden symbolism that is locked within the image that Silbury creates – the mountain mother, the divine seed and holy egg that rises out of the primeval waters.

The earliest recorded spelling of Silbury is *Seleburgh* dating from the thirteenth century AD.[13] Burgh is an Anglo-Saxon word that means mound or hill, but 'Sele' and 'Sil' pose problems, as J.E.B. Gover highlights: 'Unluckily we have very little to go upon in the interpretation of this name.'[14] Michael Dames concludes that Silbury means harvest or first fruits hill, which he traces from the Old Norse *Saell* meaning Happy, that translates as 'season' in English.[15] The names of some of the fields and rivers in the Avebury area date back to the Bronze Age, and when considering place-name origins it is important to take into account that the Celtic tongue of Welsh was the predominant language of Wiltshire countryfolk well into the eleventh century.[16] In Welsh Sil means 'seed' so Silbury could be viewed not only as harvest or first fruits hill, but as the universal seed, or giant acorn, ready to spring forth into the mighty World Tree. Seeds were often pressed into specially created holes in goddess figurines and trees were depicted growing from the belly of the Goddess.[17] The connection between the Goddess and the Sacred Tree was a central theme in the mythology of ancient cultures. In Egypt, the sycamore tree of the south was considered to be the body of the veiled Neith, an ancient goddess who was coloured green and was known as the Oldest One; her hieroglyphic sign was a cobra.[18] Neith was the Great Green Goddess, the serpent and the tree and to the Neolithic farmers in Wiltshire, so was Silbury Hill.

Silbury was the hill associated with the first fruits, and ancient Greek authors frequently wrote of a nation of people they called the 'Hyperboreans' who sent gifts of first fruits to the island of Delos. The sacred offerings were bound by a wheat straw and sent firstly to Dodona, the oldest oracle in Greece. The priesthood of Dodona known as *Selli*, were entrusted to forward the first fruits to Delos.[19] The Hyperboreans or 'dwellers beyond the north wind' had a sophisticated long-standing religious order who were intimately connected with Delos and Delphi. In Grecian mythology Latona the Hyperborean gave birth to Apollo, the god of light, under a palm tree at Delos. The etymology of Apollo's name is uncertain but it is highly probable that he too originated in Hyperborea. When Apollo was born, Zeus gave him a chariot drawn by swans in which he was to travel to Delphi, but the swans carried him to the land of the Hyperboreans instead. Who were the Hyperboreans?

Diodorus Siculus, a Roman writer, gives an account which he took from the ancient historian Hecateus (sixth century BC):

Opposite to the coast of Gallia Celtica there is an island in the ocean, not smaller than Sicily – lying to the North, which is inhabited by the Hyperboreans, who are so named because they dwell beyond the north wind. This island is of a happy temperature, rich in soil, and fruitful in every thing, yielding its produce twice in the year.[20]

It has long been recognized that this is a description of Britain. In the south-west of Britain two crops of pasture were produced as a result of water meadows, and the Druids of Britain and Ireland aptly fit the bill of the established religious order. John Matthews says that it was an ancient Bardic custom to use a wheat straw to bind a contract or covenant between two parties.[21] Diodorus writes that the Hyperboreans had a 'remarkable temple of a round form, adorned with many consecrated gifts,' and a magnificent precinct and city sacred to Apollo. The circular temple certainly sounds like a description of Stonehenge, and no doubt Apollo the god of light was associated with the monument at some stage as Stonehenge was primarily concerned with the sun's annual movements. Could the city/precinct have been the Avebury/Silbury complex, and if so how was Apollo connected to those particular sites?

The Silbury mound is a representation of the belly of the Goddess and its circular flat-topped summit is the navel, or omphalos. Silbury invites procession and the path that winds around it has appeared on all the earliest drawings of the hill, so it has existed for hundreds of years. Perhaps the path is thousands of years old and it served both a practical function as a ceremonial walkway to the hill's summit, and an iconographic function – prior to the construction of the Avebury avenues – as the meandering serpent across the huge omphalos containing the divine seed and primordial egg.

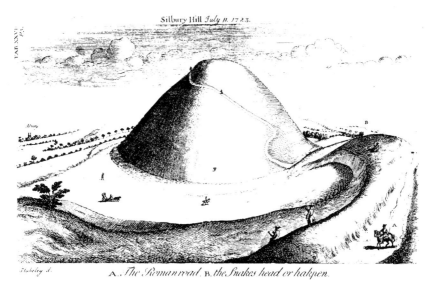

Silbury Hill with serpentine path — the omphalos of Britain.

The Neolithic communities of Wiltshire would have seen Silbury as the navel of the world, the mythical centre of the earth. The Greeks deemed Delphi to be the navel of the world. Zeus wished to discover the whereabouts of the centre of the earth and so he let loose two eagles of equal speed at the same time, from the eastern and western edges of the world. The eagles crashed together at Delphi, which became the most famous oracle of ancient Greece. Delphi was associated with the god Apollo but it was originally dedicated to the Earth Goddess Gaia, and the serpent Python was the guardian of her shrine. The word Delphi derives from the Greek *delphys*, meaning 'womb'. Two cone-shaped stones representing the omphalos were held within the temple

The omphalos of Delphi with its guardian serpent Python.

precinct,[22] one of which is decorated with an encoiling serpent and the palm of Delos – an emblem of Apollo.[23] Ancient coins from Delphi depict the omphalos stone with the guardian serpent wrapped around it in this manner.

Jane Harrison has already identified the omphalos stone as a stone that has been carved 'in the form of a tumulus',[24] but a further dimension is the stone's startling resemblance to Silbury Hill and its serpentine pathway. Silbury is Europe's largest wholly artificial representation of Gaia the Earth Goddess – the womb from which all life sprouts; Avebury is the guardian serpent Python. The descendants of Apollo's swans can still be seen gliding on the glistening waters around Silbury every winter – the seasonal period that heralded the return of the native Apollo to the Hyperboreans.

What was Apollo's mythical connection with Avebury? Apollo was the god of light and his arrows were the rays of the sun that he fired to quicken growth, but there was one specific arrow that he gave to the Hyperboreans. It was the arrow with which he had killed the Cyclops, and the task of hiding it he entrusted to the Hyperboreans. Diodorus Siculus informs us that when Abaris the Druid visited Greece he exhibited the arrow to Pythagoras at the Olympic games. Godfrey Higgins says: 'Under this story, there is evidently some allegory concealed, which I do not pretend to understand'.[25] Welsh manuscripts record that the Druids had a sacred sign called the *Nod Cyvrin* in Welsh, meaning 'Secret Mark', that later became known as 'the Broad Arrow.'[26] The Druidic or Runic Nod is comprised of three diverging lines /I\ which are the first three rays of light that radiate from the sun down to earth; from the one light, three lights emerge. The lines represent the three letters I.A.O.

that denote the Ineffable Word, the Logos. The letters of the *Coelbren y Beirdd*, or Bardic Alphabet, were cut on wood either obliquely or transversely, and the three lines that formed the Nod contained every element of the ancient Bardic Alphabet.[27] Abaris did not exhibit a physical arrow to Pythagoras, he revealed the Druidic Nod (Broad Arrow) to him; an arcane symbol that was associated with the light of the sun and therefore with Apollo. Amazingly, this holy mark was carved on stone 8 in the South Circle at Avebury!

The Nod features in many stories about the Ineffable Word, of which the legends of Robin Hood are a good example. The Sheriff of Nottingham, desperate to entrap the outlawed Robin Hood, organizes an archery contest with the prize of a golden arrow as the bait. Robin cannot resist taking part so he appears in disguise. Several archers are eliminated at each round and finally the contest is between Robin and one other participant. His opponent's arrow lands in the very centre of the bull's eye and the onlookers declare that the shot cannot be surpassed. Robin takes his impeccable aim, however, and splits the archer's arrow in two, whilst Robin's undamaged arrow lands true in the bull's eye. Robin defeats the seemingly undefeatable: he wins the contest outright, and covertly displays the Runic Nod in the process. In fact, this secret sign is at the core of even earlier legends and mysteries.

The Runic Nod carved on stone 8 in the southern quadrant of the Avebury Circle.

In the Bible, God placed a mark on the forehead of Eve's son Cain that was so sacred no harm could befall him. Cain went to live in a place called the 'Land Of Nod' after receiving this symbol from God.[28] When Moses was instructed by God to lead the children of Israel out of Egypt he asked God what he should call Him. God's mysterious reply was 'I am that I am' and this was the Unutterable Word.[29] The secret name of God translates as *Iaveh* (Jehovah) which derives from *Iahvch*, an ancient form of the verb to be.[30] In Druidry The Word is denoted by /I\, the letters IAO, and the quasi-mythical bard Taliesin had the Nod emblazoned on his forehead which is intimated by his name – 'Radiant Brow'. Taliesin was discovered floating in a bag on the water and although he was a new born baby he could already speak and possessed great wisdom. He declared:

> I was for nine months
> In the womb of the hag Caridwen;
> I was originally little Gwion,
> And at length I am Taliesin. [31]

The infant Moses was discovered floating in a basket on the river and as an adult he communed with God. When Moses returned from Mount Sinai with the Ten Commandments his forehead was aglow with 'the rays of light': 'Moses wist not that the skin of his face shone'.[32] Taliesin draws parallels between himself and Moses in several of his poems; an obvious allusion to the Radiant Brow. The Greek god Apollo was also said to have had a Radiant Brow.

In the Bible John's Gospel (known as the Spiritual Gospel) opens with the announcement that 'In the beginning was the Word, and the Word was with God, and the Word was God.' He then explains that the Word became flesh in the physical form of Jesus and that He went to John the Baptist to be baptized. (The ritual of baptism was also practiced by the Druids.) Whilst John performed the sacred act the Holy Spirit descended from heaven in the form of a dove and could be seen on the Messiah's head. In Britain the living emblem of the Druidic Nod was the Wren, and in the East it was the Dove![33] The three Rays of Light in the form of a dove came down from the heavens, and the Lamb of God, whilst standing in the waters, became Christ or *Christos*, which means the 'Anointed One'. At the Virgin Mary's Annunciation the Holy Spirit alighted upon her body as a dove also. When the Holy Spirit descended in this manner the brow upon which it fell became radiant, and the Nod was displayed as inverted \\I/. This alternative form is the magical mark of the witches known as the 'Goose Foot'[34] that derived from the primeval symbol of the sacred triangle: Gateway to the Mysteries. The dove was an extremely ancient yonic emblem, and it was sacred to Isis and several other goddesses. The Sheela-na-gigs displaying their vulvas in churches are expressing the power of the inverted version of the Holy Word; this is why the Irish *gchioch* (from which gig is derived) is related to the word *gui* to pray. The Sheelas with vulvas reaching to their knees are an embodiment of the concept of kneeling to pray to the Unutterable Name. The deeper meaning of the Masonic apron is also connected with the inverted version of the Nod; the ceremonial apron is an envelope that contains the Logos.

John the Divine brings *Revelation* to a close with the phrase, 'I am Alpha and Omega, the beginning and the end.' These words describing the return of Christ are linked to the Druidic Nod, and to the Egyptian goddess Isis (Neith also, who was often confused with Isis); Plutarch translated the inscription on the front of her temple in Sais: 'I, Isis, am all that has been, that is or shall be; no mortal hath ever me unveiled'. In *The Golden Ass* by Apuleius (*c.* AD 130) the goddess Isis declares:

I am Nature, the universal Mother, mistress of all the elements, primordial child of time, sovereign of all things spiritual, queen of the dead, queen also of the immortals, the single manifestation of all gods and goddesses that are. My nod governs the shining heights of Heaven, the wholesome sea-breezes, the lamentable silences of the world below.[35]

Both Isis and Neith wore veils, and the hag goddesses of Celtic mythology were either hooded or veiled, as the word Cailleach denotes. When Moses returned from Mount Sinai his brow was so radiant that the children of Israel were afraid to look upon him lest they should become blind, and so Moses donned a veil: 'but when Moses went in before the Lord to speak with him, he took the veil off, until he came out. And he came out, and spake unto the children of Israel that which he was commanded. And the children of Israel saw the face of Moses, that the skin of Moses' face shone: and Moses put the veil upon his face again'.[36] Moses wore the veil to shield the brilliance of the Word that he had learnt; the ancient veiled goddesses were the Word personified. Robert Graves discloses that the term 'Holy Spirit' was female in Hebrew and adds: 'The male Holy Ghost is a product of Latin grammar – *spiritus* is masculine – and of early Christian mistrust of female deities or quasi-deities.'[37] The Gnostic Christians believed that the Holy Spirit was Sophia, the Virgin of Wisdom.

In the Welsh manuscripts Taliesin is emphatic that his *awen* or inspiration (in effect all that he is) was obtained through Ceridwen and her magical Cauldron. Ceridwen swallowed Gwion in the form of a grain of wheat and he was reborn from her womb as Taliesin nine months later. It was the Hag's knowledge and awesome alchemical power that created Taliesin, and it was she who bestowed the gift of prophetic speech upon him. In the poem *The Chair of Ceridwen*, the Goddess herself is the narrator, she says:

> When all the Chairs are compared
> Mine is pre-eminent.
> My Chair, my Cauldron, my Laws.
> My searching speech gives them constancy.[38]

The Chair Ceridwen is referring to is the Bardic Chair, the seat of instruction. Ceridwen was Gwion's tutor, she pushed him through various levels of attainment symbolized by the transformations he made. The end result was the creation of Taliesin – shaman, seer and Chief of the Bards. The three drops that fell from Ceridwen's cauldron became the Nod – the three rays of light and truth. In Shelley's *Hymn of Apollo* the god says: 'The sunbeams are my shafts with which I kill Deceit'. Neith also possessed arrows of Truth (as did Robin Hood) and the name of the triune goddess Brigid means 'fiery arrow',[39] which is evidently a reference to the Druidic Nod. The three letters of the Nod signify love, knowledge and truth and it was due to this principle that 'three degrees were conferred upon the Bards of the Isle of Britain.'[40]

Freemasonry is comprised of a level of symbolic degrees, a ladder of initiation that a candidate climbs. The uppermost rung is the thirty-third degree, a level achieved by those who have been initiated by the Holy Spirit, for when Christ was crucified He was thirty-three years old. In the *Gospel According to Mark*, Jesus reveals and yet also conceals His identity: this paradox is known as The Messianic Secret. The Secret cannot be recognized by Christ's miracles, but is revealed by His suffering and death. Christ was pinned to the cross by three nails, the third being driven through His crossed feet (∴). If the three nails of the Passion are placed point to point they create the ancient symbol of the Tau Cross (the Tau Cross closely resembles the letter ⊤), but more significantly, they also form the Druidic Nod. Christ is the Alpha – the

Dove that descended during His baptism at the beginning of His Messianic role (\|/).
He is also the Omega: at the end of His reign on earth the three nails of the
crucifixion formed the Runic Nod or Broad Arrow (/|\).

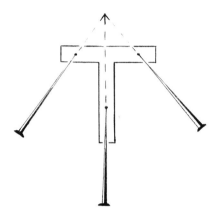

The world was redeemed by the blood that wept from the wounds in the hands,
feet and side of the Lamb of God; the Saviour hung on the cross between two thieves
and His suffering brought salvation. Christ is both aspects of the Word made flesh,
and *this* is the Messianic Secret hidden within the original Gospel of Mark before it
was adulterated by the scribes. The three nails of the crucifixion are Truth, the Whole
Truth and nothing but the Truth – the three rays of light from which Justice springs.
When a Freemason reaches the third degree he participates in a symbolic death and
resurrection ritual and is then designated a Master Mason;[41] he has been initiated
into the Mysteries and the Inner Truths.

With the Druidic Nod in mind, William Stukeley's seemingly innocent account
of how the mystery of the Avebury complex was gradually revealed to him takes on
a different light:
'When I frequented this place, which I did for some years together, to take an exact
account of it, staying a fortnight at a time, I found out the entire work by degrees.
The second time I was here, an avenue was a new amusement; the third year another.
So that at length I discovered the mystery of it.' Stukeley says he 'found out the entire
work by degrees' and implies that he discovered the mystery of Avebury during his
third year, or third degree. Stukeley was an advocate of Druidry, and also a
Freemason, and the author Paul Devereux has suggested that Stukeley's work may
contain coded phraseology.[42]

Stukeley constantly drew parallels between Avebury and Egypt and this is
interesting because the monument synonymous with Egypt is of course the pyramid,
the repository of secrets. Learned scholars such as John Michell have already
highlighted the sophisticated cabalistic numerology that was incorporated into
monuments such as the Great Pyramid.[43] Another glittering facet of the pyramidal

jewel is that when it is viewed directly from one of its edges the three visible sides of the pyramid form three diverging lines. From this perspective the geometry of the structure displays the Druidic Nod. The pyramid is, therefore, the ultimate architectural expression of the Divine Word.

The Three Rays of Light that are the Runic Nod are encoded within the architecture of the pyramids of Egypt.

The Great Pyramid has intrigued many researchers, especially the reason for its missing tip. John Michell informs us that 'At least two thousand years ago travellers reported that the last few stone courses below the summit were not in place.'[44] Was the Great Pyramid unfinished? Was the apex intact and then stolen for some reason? In his ground-breaking book *The View Over Atlantis*, John Michell suggests that the missing tip of the Great Pyramid was made of gold, and may have had a diamond or some other crystal at the apex which would 'distill the solar spark.'[45] Plato considered pyramids to be 'the element and seed of fire'; the crystal at the very tip of the Great Pyramid was the seed of fire, the allegorical mustard seed that Christ alluded to when he said:

'The kingdom of heaven is like to a grain of mustard seed, which a man took, and sowed in his field: which indeed is the least of all seeds: but when it is grown, it is the greatest among herbs, and becometh a tree, so that the birds of the air come and lodge in the branches thereof.'[46] (Matt 13:31)

The erudite hierophants of the Mystery Schools of Egypt taught the neophytes that the heavenly energies descended upon the summit of the Great Pyramid like an inverted tree, whose branches transmitted through the pyramid to earth, and the roots reached out into the universe. This analogy is Ariadne's skein of thread that will lead us out of the labyrinth, because if the Great Pyramid is viewed from a position where the crystal appears to merge with the line of the eastern horizon (referred to as the 'I' station by the Druids of Britain), the refracted rays of the rising sun create the inverted Runic Nod \I/. The pyramid itself creates the other aspect of the arcane mark /I\, and thus the monument is hermetically sealed on the line of the horizon, uniting heaven and earth.

The above comes from below, and the below from above – the work of the miracle of the One.
From the 'Emerald Tablet', attributed to Hermes Thoth Trismegistus, 'Thrice Greatest'.[47]

The sacred significance of this horizon sight line was documented in the *Koran* (XLI, 53): 'We shall show Our signs on the horizons and within themselves until it will be manifested unto them that it is the Truth.'[48] The Great Pyramid harnesses the power of the Holy Word, and radiates its brilliance out across the whole earth.

In Stukeley's *Abury* he mentions the legend of Abaris the Druid who presented the arrow of Apollo to Pythagoras, and adds that the arrow 'had been deposited in a winged temple'.[49] As we have witnessed, Avebury is the most impressive winged temple in Europe. We know that Apollo's 'arrow' was really the Logos, and so it does seem possible that Stukeley left a scattered trail of clues that lead to the Druidic Nod carved on Stone 8 at Avebury (the Runestone). The exact age of this carving is not known, but one indication of its antiquity is that it appears to have been worn smooth by hands wishing to touch the Holy Word. What *is* certain is that the entire Avebury precinct was the primary Mystery School of Britain.

CHAPTER SEVEN

CRADLE OF A NATION

I have sat in the perilous seat
Above Caer Sidi.
I shall continue to revolve
Between the three elements.

Is it not the wonder of the world
That cannot be discovered?

From *Primary Chief Bard*
(trans. John Matthews, and D.W. Nash)[1]

There are thousands of years of a continuity of tradition in the Avebury region, and the prehistoric monuments and surrounding landscape are indivisible. The monuments should not be analyzed with a myopic view for they too complement each other to form a vast architectural whole. The Avebury precinct, and the ritual landscape of the Pewsey Vale, are redolent of a way of life from which we have become so estranged. Lord Macaulay said: 'As civilization advances, poetry almost necessarily declines.' To understand the religion of prehistoric peoples is to recognize the poetic message of ancient monuments within the ceremonial landscape. Neolithic communities did not merely reserve their songs and poems for recital around the night-fire, they felt compelled to inscribe them onto the land. In this way, all their spiritual beliefs and myths were encapsulated in stone and earth, creating a Dreamtime, or Otherworld, that was actually accessible. The Druids and Bards spent many years learning these encoded myths and became the incarnate heritage of the people. Travelling the Songlines they sang the melodies of their ancestors and added the filigree to the Neolithic template. Staccato verses from these ancient anthems were recorded in the old manuscripts, but if this *mélange* of myth and legend is examined closely then a euphonic composition can be arranged.

The story of King Arthur has flourished for many centuries, and influenced countless generations of writers. Place-name associations and folklore pertaining to Arthur and his knights can be found the length and breadth of Britain. The Arthurian legends provide a tangible link with our ancient native traditions, for they contain many elements of the pagan Celtic religion. In the poem *Sir Gawain and the Green Knight*, Gawain had to seek out the Green Chapel to honour his deadly bargain with the Green Knight. The Green Chapel was a green mound situated in a valley beside a stream and 'the burn bubbled in it as though it were boiling.'[2] The Knight was waiting for Gawain inside this 'high hill'. Looking at Silbury Hill through the eyes of the Celtic Bards, Silbury becomes the Green Chapel; it was built in the valley floor of the River Kennet whilst a 'posset of milke was seething.' Perhaps the mighty horse and rider that can be seen on moonlit nights at Silbury, or the headless man also said to manifest there, is the Green Knight himself.[3] The Silbury Hag magically appearing from the flooded Winterbourne is reminiscent of the Lady of the Lake who brings forth *Caliburn*, the flaming sword of the Cally (Excalibur is the Latin corruption). The Alton Goddess is Guinevere; and even the motto of the town of Marlborough is *Ubi nunc sapientis ossa Merlini* – 'Where now are the bones of wise Merlin?', referring to the Neolithic mound in Marlborough called Merlin's Mound.

In the corpus of poems and tales related to King Arthur there is the story of his expedition to *Annwn* – the Otherworld. The *Câd Goddeu*, or 'Battle of the Trees', is an invaluable thirteenth-century Welsh minstrel poem that is about a battle between two gods for the religious control of Annwn – the British Otherworld. Was Annwn a mythical place, or could it have been a real location?

The ancient poems and tales were often loosely based on actual events and places, describing historical characters that over time inevitably gained divine attributes. The poems were also centred around the gods and goddesses of the polytheistic Celtic religion who were eventually euhemerized. Discerning myth from history and pseudo-history is, therefore, a complicated task. In addition, the poems also contain a sophisticated, secret language outlining the Bardic Mysteries and shamanic practices, along with oblique references to ancient sites; the *Câd Goddeu* is one such poem.[4] The *Câd Goddeu* was written in a deliberately obfuscated style in order to conceal various aspects of the Druidic secret doctrine contained within it. Robert Graves deciphers the poem at length in his classic text *The White Goddess*, building on the foundation laid by Reverend Edward Davies in his *Celtic Researches* (1809), that the 'Battle of the Trees' was a battle of letters of the learned connected with the Druidic Mysteries.

The *Câd Goddeu* was described in the ancient Welsh *Triads* as being one of the 'Three Frivolous Battles of Britain'.[5] There is an account of the battle in the *Myvyrian Archaiology*:

'And therefore Amathaon ap Don, and Arawn, King of Annwn, fought. And there was a man in that battle, who unless his name were known could not be overcome and there was on the other side a woman called Achren ('Trees'), and unless her name were known her party could not be overcome.'[6] The woman present at the Battle of the Trees was the Goddess – the Muse of the poets who already knew the outcome. Amathaon was the victor because Gwydion, a member of his party, guessed that the name of the unknown man in the battle was Bran, the ancient god-king of Britain. Gwydion sang:

Sure-hoofed is my steed in the day of battle:
The high sprigs of alder are in thy hand:
Bran thou art, by the branch thou bearest–
Amathaon the Good has prevailed.[7]

Robert Graves points out that Professor Sir John Rhys equates Gwydion with Woden/Odin, the Teutonic high god.[8] Graves says that Amathaon was Bran's cousin, and after forming an alliance with Gwydion (Woden) he betrayed both his cousin and his kinsmen by disclosing that Bran's sacred tree was the alder.[9] Woden was then able to usurp Bran, and the religious system of Woden replaced that of Bran.

The name Gwydion is an anagram of Wodin-Yg and *Yg* or *Yggr* was one of Woden's numerous epithets; *Ygg*drasill was Odin's sacred tree. The word Yggdrasil means, 'the World Tree that is the horse of Yggr', which is a reference to Woden 'riding' the tree when he hung on it for nine days and nights before snatching up the runes. If Bran's party had guessed Gwydion's secret name, or if they had noticed that Gwydion's sure-hoofed steed was Sleipnir, a mighty eight-legged horse (Woden's magical steed), they would have vanquished their foes, perhaps singing:

Sure-hoofed is thy steed in the day of battle:
Woden thou art, for thy steed *is* the branch thou bearest–
Bran the Blessed has prevailed.

Robert Graves deduced that Annwn was in Wiltshire, and suggested that the 'Battle of the Trees' took place at Avebury – the most likely location to have been the shrine of Bran.[10] Many of the unhewn stones of Avebury have zoomorphic and anthropomorphic characteristics; natural faces can be seen emerging out of pitted, holey recesses, and no doubt the Neolithic people carefully chose those particular sarsens for the simulacra they contained. Paul Devereux aptly describes the stones of Avebury as 'Dreamstones'[11] because of this quality. The left entrance stone of the southern circle has a natural ledge like a seat and is nicknamed 'The Devil's Chair': one of the few stones to have remained undisturbed since it was erected. Thousands of tourists have had their snapshot taken whilst sitting on the ledge of this stone. The shadowy profile of the god-king Bran can actually be perceived in the folds of the Chair. Moreover, Olaus Borrichius, a Danish scholar, noted in his journal that the tallest stone at Avebury was called the 'King-Stool', derived from the Danish *Kongstolon* or 'King's Throne'.[12] This he had learnt during an interview in 1663 with the antiquarian Walter Charleton, the royal physician to Charles II, who had studied both Stonehenge and Avebury. The largest megalith of the Avebury complex is the Devil's Chair, and it has a natural ledge like a seat so it must be the 'King's Throne' that Borrichius is referring to. This portal stone bears the stereotypical image of a god-king within it, and it was undoubtedly, at one time, the Seat of the mighty god-king Bran.

The shadowy profile of a king can be seen in the Devil's Chair (or King's Throne),
Avebury.

Avebury is a treasury of poetic myth, and the King's Throne – erroneously labelled the Devil's Chair – could equally be viewed as the 'Siege Perilous' – the unoccupied seat at King Arthur's Round Table. Sir Galahad, bearer of Joseph of Arimathea's shield, was the true Knight of God and it was his fate to sit in the perilous seat. The one whose destiny it was to sit in the Siege Perilous would fulfil the Grail prophecy, and Galahad did indeed restore the Grail to its rightful place for the honour of Christ – the purest of hearts and the King of Kings.

The apotheosized bard Taliesin claims to have sat 'in the perilous seat' and informs us that it is situated above *Caer Sidi* (the 'Revolving Castle'). Caer Sidi is another term for Annwn, and it is related to the Irish word *sidhe* meaning 'mound'.[13] The Revolving Castle was also known as the 'Spiral Castle'. Robert Graves says:

'I take Silbury to be the original Spiral Castle of Britain, as New Grange is of Ireland; the oracular shrine of Bran as New Grange was of The Dagda'.[14] Ceridwen's Cauldron of Inspiration was housed at the Revolving/Spiral Castle, and so if Silbury *is* the Spiral Castle then the Hooded Water Meadow Hag overseeing the Silbury mound becomes Ceridwen brooding over her upturned cauldron – the font of poetic wisdom and rebirth. Ceridwen shapeshifted into a hen and swallowed the grain that was Gwion, which, as Miranda Green has recognized, is an allegory of the seed buried within the womb of the earth for regeneration;[15] Silbury manifests all of these aspects.

When Taliesin speaks of the 'perilous seat' that is above *Caer Sidi* he is referring to the King's Throne at Avebury, on the high ground above Silbury Hill. In the poem 'The Defence of the Chair' Taliesin reports that Caer Sidi is surrounded by 'three circles of fire', and in 'The Spoils of Annwn' he mentions 'the four-cornered enclosure' in relation to Caer Sidi.[16] The Avebury Dragon/Serpent that coils protectively around Silbury Hill consists of three circles of stones, and the henge that encloses the megaliths has four entrance causeways. There was also a miraculous well in Annwn, and a pack of white hounds with red ears. William Stukeley recorded the existence of a herb with healing properties called *Apium nodiflorum* that grew at Swallowhead spring. He says: 'the country people have a particular regard for herbs growing there, and a high opinion of their virtue.' Apium was used to cure eye infections and it still grows in the water of Swallowhead spring; Swallowhead is the magical well whose curative waters enable sore eyes to see the Otherworld. The Hounds of Annwn also roam the Avebury precinct, as there is the legend of a white hound with red ears entering West Kennet long barrow at the summer solstice.

In the old tales and poems the Revolving Castle/Annwn could be reached through an entrance in a spring, or a gateway that was situated in another valley. Alton is that other valley, and the Land of Ann the Goddess; it is the Gateway to Annwn – the Avebury/Silbury complex. There is a gap in the Wansdyke near Adam's Grave that was called the 'Red Gate' on the Saxon charters. The gap is where the Ridgeway crosses the Wansdyke, and looking north from this point Silbury Hill can be seen. The colour red was a euphemism for the Otherworld: the red ears of the white hounds of Annwn were an indication of their Otherworldly status, and the earth at the Red Gate, now known as Red Shore, is actually red. The Saxon charters also mention a track near Adam's Grave that runs to 'Woden's Gate'.[17] The Neolithic long barrow on the breast of the Alton Goddess was known to the Saxons as Woden's Grave, and the Wansdyke was Woden's Ditch. Bonney stated that the concentration of Woden names in Alton was the result of two possibilities – either that the pagan Saxons created a sanctuary sacred to Woden that was connected with the construction of the Wansdyke; or, that a sanctuary already existed there, 'that the district became a centre of Woden's cult, and that the dyke simply acquired its name by association.'[18] The latter is most definitely the case, and once the Saxons had defeated the Britons Woden's name was attached to the Alton Goddess. This amount of Woden association in one particular area is an indication of Woden's victory at the 'Battle of the Trees', and it is logical to assume that the battle took place at the Gates to Annwn, in order to establish the right to gain entrance to the prized temple precinct of Avebury. Robert Graves was indeed correct when he surmised that Annwn was Avebury, but the battle was also associated with the Gates of Annwn – the Alton Goddess; she was the woman, who cannot lose, who was present at the 'Battle of the Trees'. Her name 'Achren' is a synonym for the Otherworld (Annwn),[19] and is further confirmation that the Alton Goddess *is* the Gateway to Annwn.

The Battle of the Trees was said to have occurred on account of a dog, a lapwing and a white roebuck from Annwn, so what part did they play? The poetic meaning of all three totemic animals is 'Guard the Secret', which is a reference to a great secret that is hidden within the poem itself.[20] The Dog was a trusted companion of many ancient gods and goddesses, it could always be relied upon to be a stalwart guardian. The Hounds of Annwn would allow the opportune adventurer to enter the Otherworld, but it was virtually impossible for him to ever leave. The Lapwing was a pseudonym for the Wren or the Dove, the Holy Word as it descends from the heavens. In the *Koran*, the lapwing was the storehouse of King Soloman's secrets.[21] The female lapwing has been known to pretend to have a broken wing, ingeniously inviting capture to lure would-be nest-robbers away from her eggs, and in the *Câd Goddeu* she helps to disguise the whereabouts of the Secret. The White Roebuck was a clever decoy in many tales and legends, he led his pursuers into the gloomy grove and always managed to befool them and evade capture. In the *Câd Goddeu* we can chase the roebuck through the enchanted forest, catching tantalizing glimpses of its white fur dashing through the dense canopy of trees; but just when the roebuck is within our grasp we notice that it has led us straight to the baying Hounds of Annwn! We are now the roebuck, cornered by the hounds and trapped in a briar of words; in order to escape we must analyze several of the tales in more detail.

In the stories of King Arthur, Bran appears as King Brandegore (Arthur's opponent), Sir Brandel (Arthur's ally), and as Uther Ben (Arthur's father).[22] Uther Ben means 'wonderful head', which is a reference to Bran's head that continued to sing and prophesy for many years after severence from his body. King Arthur returned from his quest for the cauldron of Annwn with only seven men, amongst them Taliesin. The cauldron Arthur coveted was Ceridwen's Cauldron of Inspiration and this expedition was later to become the quest for the Holy Grail. King Bran possessed a magical cauldron (Ceridwen's cauldron), and following a battle in Ireland he was mortally wounded and returned to Britain with only seven men, Taliesin being one of them. Seven of Arthur's men survived Arthur's last battle at Camlann, one of whom was Ceridwen's son Morfran, also known as Afaggdu, and Taliesin possessed the gift of poetic speech that was intended for him.

Throughout these specific tales several thematic parallels are apparent. Arthur has the power and attributes of Bran because inevitably the young king will overcome the old; Arthur is Bran's successor and inherits his status of god-king of Britain. We can also recognize veiled references to Ceridwen, and Taliesin is connected with each one of the battles: he states that he was even present at the Battle of the Trees. The number seven is a recurring motif: it is the mystic number of life (also Apollo's sacred number), and it is the sop to give to Cerberus, the honey-cake that we can feed to the hounds so that we may pass by them unharmed.

In the poem 'The Spoils of Annwn', Taliesin gives Annwn (Avebury) a new synonym seven times – Caer Sidi (also called Caer Wydr), Caer Pedryvan, Caer Vediwid, Caer Rigor, Caer Colur, Caer Vandwy and Caer Ochren. It has already been established that Caer Sidi is Silbury Hill. Peter Berresford Ellis says that Caer Wydr, or 'Glass Castle' is a Cymric synonym for the Otherworld,[23] so yet again this is a reference to Annwn, and the 'glass' aspect corresponds equally to the moat around Silbury Hill. The meaning of the six other synonyms can be ascertained by drawing on the translations of Robert Graves and John Matthews. Caer Pedryvan is the 'four cornered castle' that is connected to *Bendigeid Vran*, the Welsh for Bran the Blessed. This is a reference to the Avebury stone circle, the shrine of Bran that has four entrance causeways. Caer Vediwid or Feddwyd is 'the castle of the perfect ones', the abode of the immortals, which John Matthews equates with the hall where Bran entertained the Company of the Noble Head. Caer Rigor is a pun on the Latin *rigor mortis*, implying that this is a castle where many men perished (the area around Adam's Grave). Caer Colur or Goludd means 'the gloomy castle' or the 'Fortress of Frustration' where 'three times twenty-hundred men stood on the wall' – Wansdyke. Caer Vandwy is 'the castle on high' (the Gates to Annwn), also believed to be connected with Bran's brother, Manawydan. Caer Ochren is the castle of 'Achren', the woman in the *Câd Goddeu*. John Matthews says that Caer Ochren may at one time have been Caer Gogyrwen, which is a pun on the modern Welsh *Gogrwn*, meaning 'to riddle'.[24] Caer Ochren is indeed a riddle that refers to the Alton Goddess.

The seven synonyms are all metaphors for the various aspects of Annwn – Avebury, Silbury, the Alton Goddess and Bran the Blessed. Taliesin says that Manawydan (Bran's brother) knew the Chair of Caer Sidi well, which is why he was indirectly mentioned.[25] The allusions to Bran are riddles that all have the same answer: 'the oracular head in the King's Throne at Avebury' – the Bardic Chair situated in the national necropolis of the gods. Taliesin claims to have sat in the Seat, a practice that was part of our native shamanic tradition because the Seat provided the medium through which the deity could speak directly to the initiate. This method was also employed by the priestesses of Delphi who sat on a golden tripod (/|\) whilst Apollo imparted his prophetic wisdom through them; their divine utterances were then deciphered by the mystagogues. Dr MacCulloch proposed that there was an earlier Taliesin than the sixth-century bard, and that he was a Celtic Apollo.[26]

To interpret all of the Bardic Mysteries contained within the poems that are part of the authentic Taliesin tradition is a monumental task, one that is beyond the scope of this study. The Battle of the Trees alone is so complex that it requires a book entirely devoted to its analysis, which Robert Graves adeptly achieved in *The White Goddess*. The object of this work is to highlight that several of the poems are a map that lead to the location of Annwn; they are concerned with the Defence of Annwn, and ultimately the Cauldron of Ceridwen and the Word there interred. 'The Defence of the Chair' describes a terrible battle between the sons of Llyr, and in the poem Taliesin mentions the Chair, Caer Sidi and the Cauldron of Ceridwen. Bran was a member of the royal family of Llyr, and so this poem is a further account of the battle between Bran and his Teutonic adversary (the ally of Bran's cousin), for the religious control of Annwn – Avebury.

There are historical references to a general named Arthur who led the Britons during several battles with the Saxons in the fifth century. It appears that the Britons constructed the Wansdyke in the fifth century as a desperate attempt to prevent Saxon marauders from invading this area of Wiltshire, and it is likely that this colossal achievement was at Arthur's behest. The historical Arthur took part in several battles to stave off the Saxon advance, his last successful battle is thought to have taken place either at Barbury Castle or Liddington Castle – both of which are in Wiltshire. Researchers have been unable to identify the location of a battle that occurred near to 'Castle Guinnion'. In the Welsh *Triads* there is a place called 'Gorsedd Bryn Gwyddon' which is recorded as one of the 'primary circles of Britain'. Mr William Owen, author of the Welsh Dictionary, identified Avebury as the Gorsedd Bryn Gwyddon,[27] and this name is too similar to Castle Guinnion to be a coincidence. Nennius recorded that at the battle near Castle Guinnion 'Arthur carried on his shoulders an image of St Mary Ever-Virgin'. [28] The battle occurred near Castle Guinnion, so it did not actually take place at Avebury. The most likely location for the battle is around the Red Gate near Adam's Grave (Arthur's Strong Door to the Otherworld), with the image of the Alton Goddess right behind Arthur's shoulders!

The *Annales Cambriae* record that the battle of Camluan took place around 537-538 AD, 'in which Arthur and Modred were slain: and there was death in Britain and Ireland.'[29] In the Arthurian legends, Modred was Arthur's nephew and he instigated the battle of Camlann against Arthur in an attemp to usurp his Crown, which significantly led on to the loss of Britain's Crown to the Saxons. The Saxon Chronicles do not mention the historical Arthur but they do state that early in the year 538 AD 'the sun darkened'.[30] As Arthur the sun-king lay mortally wounded, losing his life blood on the battlefield, the sun's power waned in the heavens also, and Britain was plunged into the Dark Ages.

Arthur is mentioned in the Welsh *Triads* as one of the 'Three Frivolous Bards' of the Island of Britain, and the *Câd Goddeu* was known as one of the 'Three Frivolous Battles of Britain'. Bran was betrayed by his relative and was defeated in a religious war against the Teutonic god Woden as a result; Arthur was betrayed by his nephew and lost his life, which ineluctably led to the victory of the Saxons over the native Britons. What was the position of Arthur the general in the *mêlée*, and why are the themes within these two stories so similar that they appear to be describing the same event?

J.A. MacCulloch suggested that the Arthur saga was the 'fusing of an old Brythonic god with the historic sixth-century Arthur,' and that he 'may have been the object of a cult.'[31] Lewis Spence adds that the cult of Arthur emerged following the retreat of the Romans from Britain and that he was an old native Celtic hero-god. The Arthurian saga became the 'Gospel of Britain', the deliverance 'from Saxon invasion and oppression by a great hero-god of British origin.'[32] In Cornish legend Arthur is said to have assumed the form of a raven, and as Lewis Spence says Bran was the raven *par excellence*. Bran was rejuvenated and reinvigorated by the Druids and Bards in the form of King Arthur, at a time in Britain's history when there was a chasm that could only be bridged by a native mythical hero. As we have seen, the entire Avebury complex was the oracular shrine of Bran, and King Arthur (the new Bran) naturally inherited it. Avebury was, at one time, the primary Gorsedd of Britain, where the Druids and Bards gathered to discuss the political events of the time, to recount the ancient poems and to add new ingredients to the old formulas. Avebury became the Seat of Arthur who was the god-king and Defender of Britain, as was King Bran before him. God-kings such as Arthur and Bran were forged in the Druidic furnace, and then shaped on the anvils of the Bards during the heated rhetorical battles that took place annually at the Gorsedds. In the alchemically charged temple of Avebury (the primary Gorsedd of Britain) base metal became gold, and life was breathed into the Gods. Both the historical general Arthur and King Arthur fought the Saxons to protect the British Crown; Bran fought a spiritual battle against the Teutonic god Woden but the battles of Bran and the legendary King Arthur only ever took place in the hearts and minds of the Bards. These mythical and historical events were then grafted together and the resultant hybrid (the mystical rose) was preserved and pressed between the pages of the medieval manuscripts.

The *Câd Goddeu* is a literary masterpiece that contains a plethora of opaque references to important aspects of the ancient Mysteries of Britain, one of which is the location of Annwn. The poem records the fall of Annwn into the hands of the invading Saxons; Annwn was the heart of the nation and whoever gained control of it possessed the soul of the nation. This is why the decisive battle between the Upper Thames Saxons and the West Saxons took place at Adam's Grave, and naturally, the West Saxons defended it fiercely for as the song conveys, 'Never, since the English came to Britain was there a slaughter like the slaughter round the Great Barrow.' The two Saxon kings Ine and Ceolred fought here in 715 AD, again Annwn and the alluring cauldron of Ceridwen were hotly contested.

The veiled goddess Isis personified the secrets of the Mystery Schools of Egypt and likewise, Ceridwen personified the Mysteries of the Druidic tradition. Ceridwen's son Morfran accompanied Arthur to Annwn and his name means 'Sea-Raven' or 'Black Crow'. King Arthur's sister Morgan is equivalent to the Morrigán, a crow goddess who is also one of the Irish battle-furies, and as we have seen both Arthur and Bran had raven/crow associations. The raven or crow was originally the totem of the Crone – the territorial Hag Goddess of Celtic mythology who instilled fear on the battlefield. The significance of the crow is that, like the lapwing, it is a clever pseudonym for the wren, the emblem of the Druidic Nod. Evidence of this can be found in Ireland where the wren was linked with Bran's crow, and in Devon, one of the names for the wren is the 'cuddy vran', meaning 'Bran's sparrow'.[33] The king who chose to mate with the lascivious Hag received many blessings, one of which was the standard of the crow to prove that he possessed the Secret. Although King Arthur did not marry a hag the gallant Sir Gawain did, and this noble act saved Arthur's life and blessed his reign. The three drops from the cauldron of the Divine Hag Ceridwen created the three rays of light that form the Druidic Nod: 'from the primary utterance of which emanated all lays and melodies',[34] and these three rays can be seen at Avebury. In the 'Spoils of Annwn', Taliesin says that the cauldron has 'a ridge around its edge of pearls';[35] Silbury with its mysterious ridge is the pearl of wisdom in the Avebury landscape.

Avebury, Silbury and the Vale of Pewsey house a myriad of secrets and they are inextricably linked. The key can be turned one more notch, however, in the lock of the Gates of Annwn, and as the final lever releases the catch the gates slowly open and the canine sentinels allow us to draw back the curtain of time. It is Lughnasadh Eve and the full moon, like the Alton Goddess, is heavily pregnant. The white roebuck suddenly appears and guides us straight through the dark gateway with his seven tines of light. The elusive lapwing no longer feigns injury but beckons for us to follow, leading the way to the top of the section of the henge opposite the Runestone (stone 8) in the South Circle of Avebury. There on the bank's summit the lapwing transforms into a phoenix, and a Promethean wonder is revealed. The huge Lughnasadh bonfire on Ann's (Tan) Hill creates the subtle image of flames issuing forth from Silbury itself: this is due to Silbury's summit being aligned to Tan Hill, the highest hill in Wiltshire.[36] The Womb of the Mysteries is illuminated in glory as the Lughnasadh full moon glides across the Silbury waters, and the folk-saying that 'Silbury was raised while a posset of milk was seething' rings out true across the night air. Archæologists discovered that work began on Silbury in early August due to the presence of the winged ants in the turf. In early August, at Lughnasadh, Ceridwen's posset can be seen to seethe in the glow from the celebratory bonfire on Tan Hill, and the reflection of the full moon on Silbury's surrounding moat transmutes water into milk.

The Avebury precinct and the Pewsey Vale create a legendary land of milk and poetic honey, and express: 'All that has been, that is or shall be'.

© Crown copyright. NMR.

The Chair and Cauldron of Ceridwen
Are they without defence?
I remain tongue-tied in her enclosure,
Where, to her glory,
Milk, dew, and acorns are offered.
From 'The Defence of the Chair', one of the poems attributed to Taliesin.[37]

Notes

Introduction

1 Hartzell, Hal Jr., *The Yew Tree: A Thousand Whispers*, 1991, p. xv.
2 Lévy-Bruhl, Lucien, *Primitive Mythology*, (1935), 1983 edition, cited in Devereux, Paul, *Symbolic Landscapes: Dreamtime Earth and Avebury's Open Secrets*, 1992, p. 7.

Chapter 1
A Monumental Legacy

1 Aubrey, John, *Wiltshire: The Topographical Collections of John Aubrey*, 1659–70, ed. Canon J.E. Jackson, 1862, p. 332.
2 Whitlock, Ralph, *The Folklore of Wiltshire*, 1976, p. 23.
3 Smith, A.C., *Wiltshire Archæological Magazine*, vol. 7, 1862, p. 181.
4 Merewether, J., *Diary of a Dean*, 1851, p. 35.
5 Burl, Aubrey, *The Stone Circles of the British Isles*, 1976, p. 327.
6 Dames, Michael, *The Silbury Treasure: The Great Goddess Rediscovered*, 1976, pp. 52–8.
7 Massingham, H.J., *The Wisdom of the Fields*, cited in Watts, Kenneth, *The Marlborough Downs*, 1993, p. 27.
8 Watts, Kenneth, *op. cit.*, p. 88.
9 Wiltshire, Kathleen, *Wiltshire Folklore*, 1975, p. 60.
10 Watts, Kenneth, *op. cit.*, p. 27.
11 Grinsell, Leslie V., *Folklore of Prehistoric Sites in Britain*, 1976, p. 113.
12 *Ibid.*, p. 117.
13 Hoare, Sir R.C., *The Ancient History of North Wiltshire*, 1819, pp. 11–12.
14 Dennis, I. and Hamilton, M.A., *Exploratory excavations and survey of Mesolithic, Late Bronze Age and Iron Age sites at Golden Ball Hill, near Alton Barnes*, 1997.

Chapter 2
Peering Through The Veil

1 The excerpt from the 'Song of Amergin' is a translation by Robert Graves in *The White Goddess*, 1961, p. 13. Graves explains that 'The Song of Amergin' was said to have been chanted in 1268 BC by the chief bard of the Milesian invaders when he first stepped onto Irish soil. The poem contains a coded calendar alphabet; for a detailed analysis see pp. 205–22 of *The White Goddess*.
2 Windels, Fernand, *The Lascaux Cave Paintings*, 1950, p. 52, cited in Streep, Peg, *Sanctuaries of The Goddess*, 1994, p. 26.
3 Meaden, Terence, *Stonehenge: The Secret of the Solstice*, 1997, pp. 19–20.
4 Hutton, Ronald, *Pagan Religions of the Ancient British Isles*, 1991, pp. 1–3.
5 Ferguson, Diana, *The Magickal Year*, 1996, p. 16.
6 Gimbutas, Marija, *The Goddesses and Gods of Old Europe*, 1982, p. 235.
7 Scully, Vincent, speaking of ancient sites in Greece in *The Earth, The Temple and the Gods*, 1962, pp. 2–5.
8 Michell, John, *Simulacra*, 1979, p. 29.
9 Dames, Michael, commenting on Vincent Scully's study of temples in Greece and Crete in *The Avebury Cycle*, 1996 edition, p. 125.
10 Baring Gould, S., *Lives of the British Saints*, vol. I, 1907, p. 164.
11 Broadhurst, Paul, *Secret Shrines: In Search of the old Holy Wells of Cornwall*, 1988.
12 Graves, Robert, *The White Goddess*, 1961, p. 371.

13 *Ibid.*, p. 372.
14 Pugh, R.B., in *Collection Charter Rolls* 1427-1516, vol. 4, p. 273.
15 Story-Maskelyne,T., *Wiltshire Archæological Magazine*, vol. 34, 1905, p. 426.
16 *Ibid.*
17 Thurnam, J., *Wiltshire Archæological Magazine*, vol. 4, 1858, p. 324.
18 MacNeill, Máire, *The Festival of Lughnasa*, 1962, p. 388.
19 Story-Maskelyne,T., *op. cit.*, p. 430.
20 Baring Gould, S., Brittany, cited in Story-Maskelyne,T., *op. cit.*, p. 430.
21 Wiltshire, Kathleen, *Wiltshire Folklore*, 1975, p. 59.

Chapter 3
Adam, Eve and Serpent

1 Excerpt from the thirteenth century Welsh minstrel poem the *Câd Goddeu*, ('The Battle of the Trees'), from a translation by Matthews, John in *Taliesin: Shamanism and the Bardic Mysteries in Britain and Ireland*, 1991, p. 299.
2 Gover, J.E.B., *Place Names of Wiltshire*, 1939.
3 Northcote Toller, T., *Anglo-Saxon Dictionary*, 1898.
4 Smith A.C., *Guide to the British and Roman Antiquities of the North Wiltshire Downs*, 1885, p. 187.
5 *Ibid.*, p. 188.
6 Cyriax, T., in *Archæological Journal*, vol. 28, 1921, pp. 205–15, cited in Dames, Michael, *The Avebury Cycle*, 1996, p. 30.
7 Gimbutas, Marija, *The Civilization of the Goddess,* 1991, p. 281.
8 *Ibid.*
9 Gimbutas, Marija, *The Language of the Goddess*, 1989, p. 153.
10 Hoare, Sir R.C., *op. cit.*, p. 111.
11 Leach, Maria, (ed.) *Funk and Wagnalls Standard Dictionary of Folklore, Mythology, and Legend*, 1984, p. 75.
12 Malone, Caroline, *Avebury*, 1989, p. 74.
13 Burl, Aubrey, *Prehistoric Avebury*, 1979, p. 102.
14 *Ibid.*, p. 217.
15 *Ibid.*, p. 123.
16 Jordan, Katharine, *The Folklore of Ancient Wiltshire*, 1990, p. 31.
17 Watts, Kenneth, *op. cit.*, p. 64.
18 Bonney, D.J., 'The Pagan Saxon Period', in *Victoria County History*, vol. I, p. 479.
19 Frazer, Sir James, *The Worship of Nature*, vol. I, 1926, p. 318.
20 The Wansdyke is recorded on a medieval road map as the 'Devill's Ditch', cited in Major, Albany F. and Burrow, Edward J., *The Mystery of Wansdyke*, 1926, p. 6.
21 Jeffrey, David Lyle, *A Dictionary of Biblical Tradition in English Literature*, 1992, p. 16.
22 Leach, Maria, *op. cit.*, pp. 983–95.
23 Graves, Robert, *The White Goddess*, 1990, p. 257.
24 Jeffrey, David Lyle, *op. cit.*, p. 15.
25 Morgan, Morien, *The Mabin of the Mabinogion*, 1984 edition, p. 236.
26 Jeffrey, David Lyle, *op. cit.*, p. 252.
27 Thurnam, Dr, *Wiltshire Archæological Magazine*, vol. 6, 1853–57, p. 326.
28 Goddard, Rev E.H., *Wiltshire Archæological Magazine*, vol. 38, 1913, p. 163.
29 Cunnington, M.E.,'Knap Hill', *Wiltshire Archæological Magazine*, vol. 37, 1912, p. 43.
30 Goddard, Rev E.H., *op. cit.*, p. 163.
31 Cunnington, M.E., *op. cit.*, p. 45.
32 *Ibid.*, p. 46.
33 Connah, Graham, 'Excavations at Knap Hill, Alton Priors 1961', *Wiltshire Archæological Magazine*, vol. 60, 1965, p. 2.

34 Johnson, Buffie, *Lady of the Beasts*, 1994, p. 124.
35 *Ibid.*, p. 172.
36 Stukeley, William, *Abury Described*, 1742, p. 93.
37 *Ibid.*, p. 96.
38 Cunnington, M.E., *op. cit.*, p. 49.
39 *Ibid.*, p. 48.
40 Meaden, Terence, *op. cit.*, p. 48.
41 Gimbutas, Marija, T*he Language of the Goddess*, 1989, p. 237.
42 Burl, Aubrey, *Prehistoric Avebury*, 1979, p. 101.
43 Smith, I.F., *Windmill Hill and Avebury: A Short Account of the Excavations*, 1959, p. 3.
44 Dyer, James, *Southern England, an Archæological Guide*, 1973, p. 328.
45 Cunnington, M.E., *op. cit.*, p. 62.
46 *Ibid.*, pp. 62–3.
47 Hippisley Cox, R., *Where Green Roads Meet*, 1929, p. 7.
48 Hoare, Sir. R.C., *op. cit.*, p. 57.
49 Stukeley, William, *Abury Described*, 1743, p. 18.
50 Burl, Aubrey, *Prehistoric Avebury*, p. 50.
51 Michell, John, *Megalithomania*, 1982, p. 14.
52 Burl, Aubrey, *op. cit.*, p. 51.

Chapter 4
All the World's A Stage
(From William Shakespeare's *As You Like It*)

1 Dames, Michael, *The Silbury Treasure*, 1976, pp. 166–76.
2 MacNeill, Máire, *op. cit.*, p. 10.
3 *Ibid.*, p. 420.
4 Lambeth, M., *A Golden Dolly*, 1969, p. 99.
5 Hone, William, *The Every Day Book*, vol. II, 1826, cited in Hole, Christina, *A Dictionary of British Folk Customs*, 1976, pp. 136–7.
6 Ferguson, Diana, *The Magickal Year*, 1996, p. 171.
7 *Ibid.*
8 Gimbutas, Marija, *The Language of the Goddess*, 1989, p. 149.
9 Green, Miranda, *Celtic Goddesses*, 1995, p. 114.
10 Leach, Maria, *op. cit.*, p. 642.
11 *Ibid.*
12 MacNeill, Máire, *op. cit.*, pp. 316–19.
13 Hole, Christina, *op. cit.*, p. 137. Hole records that this practice is still observed at Whalton, Northumberland and at Little Waltham, Essex.
14 Wright, A.R. and Jones, T.E., *British Calendar Customs, England*, vol. 3, 1936, p. 47, reported by Miss J.B. Partridge in 1908.
15 Story-Maskelyne, T., *op. cit.*, p. 426.
16 MacNeill, Máire, *op. cit.*, p. 104.
17 Graves, Robert, *op. cit.*, p. 103.
18 Hutton, Ronald, *The Stations of the Sun*, 1996, p. 381.
19 Hole, Christina, *op. cit.*, p. 150.
20 Farrar, Janet and Russell, Virginia, *The Magical History of the Horse*, 1992, p. 89.
21 Stukeley, William, *Itinerarium Curiosum*, vol. I., 1724, pp. 131–2.
22 Jordan, Katharine, *op. cit.*, p. 47.
23 Bayley, Adrian, *The Caves of the Sun*, 1997, pp. 63–5.
24 Hicks, R. E. *Some Henges and Hengiform Earthworks in Ireland*, 1975, p. 195, PHD diss., University of Pennslyvania. Cited in Burl, Aubrey, *The Stone Circles of the British Isles*, 1976, p. 241.

25 Whitlock, Ralph, *In Search of Lost Gods*, 1979, p. 177.
26 Muir, Frank and Jamie, *A Treasury of Christmas*, 1991 editon, p. 25.
27 Whitlock, Ralph, *Wiltshire Folklore*, 1976, p. 71.
28 Muir, Frank and Jamie, *op. cit.*, p. 23.
29 Clare, John, *Poems, descriptive of Rural Life and Scenery*, cited in Muir, Frank and Jamie, *op. cit.*, p. 45.
30 Carmichael, Alexander, *Carmina Gadelica*, vol. I, 1900, pp. 169–71.
31 *Ibid.*, p. 172.
32 Trevelyan, Marie, *Folk-Lore and Folk-Stories of Wales*, 1909, pp. 22–4.
33 MacCulloch, J.A., *The Religion of the Ancient Celts*, 1911, p. 266.
34 Slade, Paddy, *Natural Magic*, 1990, p. 92.
35 Dames, Michael, *The Avebury Cycle*, 1977, p. 196.
36 Watts, Kenneth, *op. cit.*, p. 30.
37 Collectanae, in *Folklore*, vol. 20, 1909, p. 8.
38 Partridge, J.B. in *Folklore*, vol. 26, 1915, p. 211.
39 Timperley, H.W., *The Vale of Pewsey*, 1954, p. 189.
40 Green, H.J.M., *Pagan Gods and Shrines of the Roman Empire*, ed. Martin Henig and Anthony King, 1986, p. 49.
41 *Ibid.*
42 Hendrickson, Robert, *Encyclopedia of Word and Phrase Origins*, 1987, p. 350.
43 Ferguson, Diana, *op. cit.*, p. 110.
44 Hole, Christina, *op. cit.*, p. 193.
45 *Ibid.*, p. 194.
46 Hutton, Ronald, *The Stations of the Sun*, 1996, p. 259.
47 Leach, Maria, *op. cit.*, p. 534.
48 The anthropologist Lady Raglan was the first to coin the phrase 'the Green Man' in her influential article, 'The Green Man in Church Architecture', *Folklore*, vol. 50, 1939, pp. 45–57.
49 Basford, Kathleen, *The Green Man*, 1978, p. 9.
50 Anderson, J.J., (ed.) *Sir Gawain and the Green Knight*, 1996, pp. 172–86.
51 Millson, Cecilia, *Tales of Old Wiltshire*, 1995, p. 71.
52 Whitlock, Ralph, *In Search of Lost Gods*, 1979, p. 184.

Chapter 5
The Hag of Silbury Hill

1 Gimbutas, Marija, *The Language of the Goddess*, 1989, p. 206.
2 Dames, Michael, *The Avebury Cycle*, 1996, p. 33.
3 *Ibid.*, p. 34.
4 Thurnam, J., 'Examination of a chambered long barrow at West Kennet, Wiltshire', in *Archæologia*, vol. 38, 1860.
5 Stukeley, William, *Itinerarium Curiosum*, vol. I, 1723, p. 63.
6 Davis, T., *General View of the Agriculture of the County of Wiltshire*, 1794, p. 30.
7 Atwood, George, *Wiltshire Archæological Magazine*, vol. 58, 1963, p. 410.
8 *Ibid.*
9 Aubrey, John, *Natural History of Wiltshire*, 1656–91, p. 104.
10 Davis, T., *op. cit.*, p. 30.
11 From a report by Wessex Archæology, The Proposed Burial of 11KV Power Cables at Avebury, *Wiltshire: Archæological Evaluation of the Silbury Hill Section*, 1996.
12 Dimbleby, G.W., *Ecology and Archæology*, 1977, p. 32, cited in Dillon, Patrick J., *A Case Study of Silbury Hill, Wiltshire*, 1981.
13 Gover, J.E.B., *Place Names of Wiltshire*, 1939, p. 295.
14 Gimbutas, Marija, *The Civilization of the Goddess*, 1991, p. 305.
15 Ross, Anne, 'The Divine Hag of the Pagan Celts', *The Witch Figure*, ed. Venetia Newall, 1973, p. 146.
16 Matthews, John, *Taliesin: Shamanism and the Bardic Mysteries in Britain and Ireland*, 1991, p. 3.

17 *Sanas Chormaic*, trans. O'Donovan, John and ed. Whitley, Stokes, 1868.
18 Ellis Davidson, H.R., *Viking and Norse Mythology*, 1996, p. 65.
19 Matthews, John, *Taliesin*, p. 244.
20 Macleod, Fiona, *Poems and Dramas*, 1912, p. 153.
21 Leach, Maria, *op. cit.*, p. 473.
22 Condren, Mary, *The Serpent and The Goddess*, 1989, p. 82.
23 Brooke, Charlotte, *Reliques of Irish Poetry*, 1789, pp. 70–1, cited in Dames, Michael, *Mythic Ireland*, 1992, p. 55.
24 Patterson, T.G.F., 'Folk tales from Creggan parish', *Ulster Journal of Archæology*, vol. I, 1938, p. 36. Cited in Dames, *Mythic Ireland*, p. 55.
25 Dames, Michael, *op. cit.*, p. 55.
26 Straffon, Cheryl, *The Earth Goddess*, 1997, p. 46.
27 *Ibid.*
28 Ross, Anne, *Pagan Celtic Britain*, 1974, p. 160.
29 *Antiquity*, vol. 58, 1985–86, p. 52.
30 *Ibid.*
31 *Ibid.*
32 Leach, Maria, *op. cit.*, p. 180.
33 Patterson, T.J.F., 'Harvest Customs', *Ulster Journal of Archæology*, vol. 7, 1944, pp. 114–5. Cited in Dames, *Mythic Ireland*, p. 56.
34 Wilkinson, Rev J., *Wiltshire Archæological Magazine*, vol. II, 1869, p. 113.
35 Frazer, J.G., in *Folklore*, vol. 7, 1896, p. 51.
36 Leach, Maria, *op. cit.*, p. 180.
37 *Ibid.*
38 Hole, Christina, *op. cit.*, p. 149.
39 *Ibid.*, p. 336.
40 Carmichael, Alexander, *op. cit.*, p. 149.
41 *Ibid.*
42 Matthews, John, *Taliesin*, 1991, p. 113.
43 Hole, Christina, *op. cit.*, p. 65.
44 *Ibid.*
45 *Ibid.*, p. 66.
46 Ferguson, Diana, *op. cit.*, p. 54.
47 Guerber, H.A., *Myths of the Norsemen*, 1909, p. 57.
48 Lurker, Manfred, *Dictionary of Gods and Goddesses, Devils and Demons*, 1987, p. 61.
49 Leach, Maria, *op. cit.*, p. 137.
50 Barnstone, Willis, *The Other Bible*, 1984, pp. 404–6.
51 *Ibid.*, p. 405.
52 *Ibid.*
53 Roberts, Jack, *The Sheela-na-Gigs of Britain and Ireland: An Illustrated Guide*, 1997.
54 *Ibid.*
55 *Ibid.*
56 Straffon, Cheryl, *op. cit.*, 1997, p. 72.
57 Anderson, Jørgen, *The Witch on the Wall*, 1977, ch. 1.
58 Weir, Anthony and Jerman, James, *Images of Lust*, 1986, p. 146.
59 Neumann, E., *The Great Mother*, 1955, p. 99.
60 Roberts, Jack, *The Sheela-na-Gigs of Britain and Ireland*, 1994, p. 22.
61 *Ibid.*
62 Weir and Jerman, *op. cit.*, p. 26.
63 Johnson, Buffie, *op. cit.*, p. 176.
64 Weir and Jerman, *op. cit.*, p. 25.
65 *Ibid.*, p. 18.

66 Ross, Anne, *Pagan Celtic Britain*, 1992, p. 346.
67 Straffon, Cheryl, *op. cit.*, p. 49.
68 *Ibid.*
69 Cross, Tom Peete and Slover, Clarke Harris, *Ancient Irish Tales*, 1996, p. 103.
70 MacNeill, Máire, *op. cit.*, p. 406.
71 *Ibid.*, p. 576.
72 *Ibid.*, p. 400.
73 Allen, Michael J. and Powell, Andrew B., Archæology in the Avebury area, *Wiltshire: A Recent Study*, 1993, p. 85.
74 *Ibid.*
75 Piggott, S., *The West Kennet Long Barrow Excavations*, 1955–6, 1963, pp. 55–6.
76 Watts, Kenneth, *op. cit.*, p. 97.
77 *The Oxford Classical Dictionary*, ed. Hammond, N.G.L. and Scullard, H.H., 1970 second edition, p. 773.
78 Leach, Maria, *op. cit.*, p. 843.
79 Ross, Anne, *op. cit.*
80 Gimbutas, Marija, *The Goddesses and Gods of Old Europe*, 1996, pp. 216–27.
81 Green, Miranda, *op. cit.*, p. 41.
82 Gloss. Spenser's Shepherds' Calendar (1579), cited in Boardman, John, *The Great God Pan: The Survival of an Image*, 1997, p. 24.
83 Heanley, Robert, 'The Devil and Silbury Hill', *Folklore*, vol. XXIV, 1913, p. 524.
84 Jordan, Katharine, *The Folklore of Ancient Wiltshire*, 1990, p. 31.
85 Burl, Aubrey, *Prehistoric Avebury*, 1979, p. 33.

Chapter 6
The Mysteries of Avebury

1 The excerpt from the poem 'The Death Song of Uther Pendragon' is a translation by Matthews, John and Caitlín in *Taliesin: Shamanism and the Bardic Mysteries in Britain and Ireland*, 1991, p. 306. The poem belongs to the authentic 'Taliesin tradition'.
2 Devereux, Paul, *op. cit.*, p. 123.
3 Dames, Michael, *The Silbury Treasure*, 1992, p. 175.
4 Hippisley Cox, R., *A Guide to Avebury and the Green Roads of England*, 1909, p. 11.
5 Timperley, H.W., *The Vale of Pewsey*, 1954, p. 215, commenting on Cunnington's findings. See also, Cunnington, M.E., *Wiltshire Archæological Magazine*, vol. 38, p. 644.
6 Cavendish, Richard, *Prehistoric England*, 1983, p. 47.
7 Burl, Aubrey, *Prehistoric Avebury*, 1979, p. 218 (moon alignment). For solar alignment see Meaden, Terence, *op. cit.*, 1997, p. 152.
8 Hippisley Cox, R. *op. cit.*, p. 55.
9 Michell, John, *The View Over Atlantis*, 1973, p. 44.
10 Keiller, Alexander and Piggott, Stuart, 'The West Kennet Avenue, Avebury', *Excavations* 1934–5, p. 4. Reprinted from *Antiquity*, vol. 10, 1936.
11 Hoare, Sir R.C., *op. cit.*, cited in Higgins, Godfrey, *The Celtic Druids*, 1829, p. xxiii.
12 Stukeley, William, *Abury Described*, 1743, p. 41.
13 Gover, J.E.B., *English Place Name Society*, vol. 16, Wiltshire, 1939, p. 295. Cited in Dames, *The Silbury Treasure*, p. 145.
14 *Ibid.*
15 Dames, Michael, *op. cit.*, pp. 144–5.
16 Deanesly, M., *The Pre-Conquest Church in England*, 1961, p. 81, cited in Burl, Aubrey, *Prehistoric Avebury*, 1979, p. 32.
17 Gimbutas, Marija, *The Language of the Goddess*, 1989, p. 103.
18 Johnson, Buffie, *op. cit.*, p. 132.
19 Klapp, Alexander S., *Murray's Manual of Mythology*, 1936, p. 38.

20 Diodorus Siculus, II:47, trans. *Oldfather, C.H.*, 1967, pp. 37–41.

21 Matthews, John, *The Druid Source Book*, 1996, p. 143.

22 *The Oxford Classical Dictionary*, ed. Hammond and Scullard, p. 752.

23 Johnson, Buffie, *op. cit.*, p. 149.

24 Harrison, Jane Ellen, *Themis: A Study in the Social Origins of Greek Religion*, 1962, p. 399, cited in Streep, Peg, *op. cit.*, p. 180.

25 Higgins, Godfrey, *op. cit.*, p. 124.

26 Morgan, Morien, *op. cit.*, pp. 93–4.

27 Guest, Lady Charlotte, *The Mabinogion*, 1906, p. 315.

28 *Genesis* 5:15–17.

29 *Exodus 3*:13–16.

30 Matthews, John, *The Druid Source Book*, 1996, p. 217.

31 Guest, Lady Charlotte, *op. cit.*, p. 274.

32 *Exodus* 35:29.

33 Morgan, Morien, *op. cit.*, p. 77.

34 Crowther, Patricia, *Lid Off the Cauldron*, 1981, p. 101.

35 Apuleius, Lucius, *The Golden Ass*, trans. by Graves, Robert, 1960, p. 190.

36 *Exodus* 35:33–35.

37 Graves, Robert, *The White Goddess*, 1961, p. 157.

38 Matthews, John, *Taliesin*, 1991, p. 64.

39 Hutton, Ronald, *Stations of the Sun*, 1996, p. 135.

40 Spence, Lewis, *The Mysteries of Britain*, 1993 reprint, p. 95.

41 Knight, Christopher and Lomas, Robert, *The Second Messiah*, 1997, p. 5.

42 Devereux, Paul, *op. cit.*, p. 155.

43 Michell, John, *The View Over Atlantis*, 1976, pp. 87–8.

44 *Ibid.*, p. 88.

45 *Ibid.*, p. 98.

46 *Ibid.*, pp. 98–9.

47 From a translation by Powell, Robert, 'Historical Note concerning the Emerald Tablet', *The Hermetic Journal*, 1981, p. 38.

48 The quote from the *Koran* was cited in Michell, John, *op. cit.*, p. 24, in relation to the ley system of aligned structures.

49 Stukeley, William, *Abury Described*, 1742, p. 97.

Chapter 7
Cradle of A Nation

1   The first four lines of the extract from 'Primary Chief Bard' are from a translation by Matthews, John, in *Taliesin*, 1991, p. 285. The last two lines are from a translation by Nash, D.W. cited in Graves, Robert, *The White Goddess*, 1961, p. 91.

2   Anderson, J.J., (ed.) *Sir Gawain and the Green Knight*, 1996, pp. 261–2.

3   Whitlock, Ralph, *The Folklore of Wiltshire*, 1976, p. 23.

4   For an in-depth analysis of the 'Battle of the Trees' and the secret alphabet see Graves, Robert, *The White Goddess*. For a comprehensive study of the Bardic shamanic teachings outlined in the poems attributed to Taliesin see Matthews, John, *Taliesin*.

5   Graves, Robert, *op. cit.*, p. 30.

6   *Ibid.*, p. 49.

7   *Ibid.*

8   *Ibid.*, p. 56.

9   *Ibid.*, p. 127.

10 *Ibid.*, p. 58.

11 See Devereux, Paul, *op. cit.*

12 Ucko, Peter J. *Avebury Reconsidered: From the 1660s to the 1990s*, 1991, pp. 23–4. Borrichius mentions the King-Stool in his journal, and in a letter to Bartholinus, and in both sources the details of the height of the Avebury stones are contradictory and confused, especially when Borrichius refers to the King-Stool. He appears to have misconstrued what Charleton told him, so it is not clear from his account exactly which stone at Avebury was called the 'King's Throne'. Ucko suggests that the King-Stool was perhaps the Obelisk, although he does say, however, that according to Stukeley 'Kingstones' were not situated within the centre of the stone circle. The Devil's Chair has a natural ledge that forms a seat, it is a portal stone so it does not lie in the centre of the circle, it has the appropriate associated name and the simulacrum of a man's face within it.

13 Graves, Robert, *op. cit.*, p. 101.

14 *Ibid.*, p. 295.

15 Green, Miranda, *op. cit.*, p. 69.

16 See Matthews, John, *Taliesin*, pp. 294–6. Taliesin refers to the four-cornered enclosure in *Preiddeu Annwn* ('The Spoils of Annwn') see Graves, Robert, *op. cit.*, 107–8.

17 See The Saxon Land Charters of Wiltshire p. 162, also *Wiltshire Archæological Magazine*, vol. LIII, p. 384.

18 Bonney, D.J., *op. cit.*, p. 479.

19 Ellis, Peter Berresford, *Dictionary of Celtic Mythology*, 1992, p. 17.

20 Graves, Robert, *op. cit.*, pp. 53–4.

21 *Ibid.*, p. 54.

22 *Ibid.*, p. 60.

23 Ellis, Peter Berresford, *op. cit.*, p. 55.

24 Matthews, John, *op. cit.*, p. 254. Pages 252–4 contain translations of the seven castles. See also Graves, Robert, *op. cit.*, p. 106.

25 See 'The Defence of the Chair' trans. Matthews, John, *op. cit.*, p. 295.

26 Graves, Robert, *op. cit.*, p. 92.

27 Long, William, *Wiltshire Archæological Magazine*, vol. 4, 1858, p. 338. Also Aubrey, John, *Wiltshire: The Topographical Collections of John Aubrey*, 1659–70, ed. Canon J.E. Jackson, 1862, p. 332.

28 Nennius, *History of the Britons*, from a translation cited in Ashe, Geoffrey, *The Quest for Arthur's Britain*, 1968, p. 40.

29 Ellis, Peter Berresford, *op. cit.*, p. 56.

30 Savage, Anne, *The Anglo-Saxon Chronicles*, 1995, p. 35.

31 MacCulloch, J.A., *The Religion of the Ancient Celts*, 1911, p. 119.

32 Spence, Lewis, *The Magic Arts in Celtic Britain*, 1945, pp. 148–9.

33 Graves, Robert, *op. cit.*, p. 186.

34 From an old manuscript in the library of Raglan Castle entitled 'The Roll of Tradition and Chronology' that was published with the Iolo Manuscripts. Cited in Matthews, John, *The Druid Source Book*, 1996, p. 219.

35 Graves, Robert, *op. cit.*, p. 108.

36 John Michell observed an alignment that extends from Tan Hill through Silbury Hill to Waden Hill/Avebury, and surmised that the Tan Hill bonfire could probably be seen above Silbury Hill somewhere along this site line.

37 The lines are from the poem 'The Defence of the Chair', from a translation by Matthews, John in *Taliesin*, p. 77.

Select Bibliography

Anderson, J.J., (ed.) *Sir Gawain and the Green Knight*, London, 1996.
Anderson, Jørgen, *The Witch on the Wall*, London, 1977.
Apuleius, Lucius, *The Golden Ass*, trans. Robert Graves, London, 1960.
Ashe, Geoffrey, *The Quest for Arthur's Britain*, London, 1968.
Atkinson, R.J.C., *Silbury Hill*, London, 1967.
— *Stonehenge and Avebury*, London, 1959.
Aubrey, John, *The Topographical Collections, 1659–70*, ed. Canon J.E. Jackson, London, 1862.
— *Monumenta Britannica*, 1665–90.
— *Natural History of Wiltshire*, 1656–91, ed. J. Britton, London, 1847.
Barnstone, Willis, *The Other Bible*, New York, 1984.
Basford, Kathleen, *The Green Man*, Cambridge, 1978.
Bayley, Adrian, *The Caves of The Sun: The Origins of Mythology*, London, 1997.
Boardman, John, *The Great God Pan: The Survival of an Image*, London, 1997.
Burl, Aubrey, *Prehistoric Avebury*, London, 1979.
— *The Stone Circles of the British Isles*, London, 1976.
Carmichael, Alexander, *Carmina Gadelica*, 2 vols, Edinburgh, 1900.
Carpenter, Edward, *The Origins of Pagan and Christian Beliefs*, London, 1996.
Carr-Gomm, Philip, (ed.) *The Druid Renaissance*, London, 1996.
Chandler, John, *The Vale of Pewsey*, Wiltshire, 1991.
Condren, Mary, *The Serpent and the Goddess*, New York, 1989.
Crawford, O.G.S., *The Eye Goddess*, London, 1957.
Cross, Tom Peete and Slover, Clarke Harris, *Ancient Irish Tales*, New York, 1996.
Curwen, E.C., 'Neolithic Camps', *Antiquity*, vol. IV, 1930.
Dames, Michael, *The Silbury Treasure*, London, 1976.
— *The Avebury Cycle*, London, 1977.
— *Mythic Ireland*, London, 1992.
Davis, T. *General View of the Agriculture of the County of Wiltshire*, London, 1794.
Devereux, Paul, *Symbolic Landscapes: Dreamtime Earth and Avebury's Open Secrets*, Glastonbury, 1992.
Dimbleby, G.W., *Ecology and Archæology*, London, 1977.
Dyer, J., *Southern England, an Archæological Guide*, London, 1973.
Ekwall, E., *English River Names*, Oxford, 1928.
Ellis Davidson, H.R., *Viking and Norse Mythology*, London, 1996.
Ellis, Peter Berresford, *The Druids*, London, 1994.
Farrar, Janet and Virginia, Russell, *The Magical History of the Horse*, London, 1992.
Ferguson, Diana, *The Magickal Year*, London, 1996.
Fowler, Peter, *Images of Prehistory*, Cambridge, 1990.

Frazer, J.G., *The Golden Bough,* London, 1922.
— *The Worship of Nature,* vol. 1, London, 1926.
Gaddon, Elinor W., *The Once and Future Goddess,* London, 1995.
Gimbutas, Marija, *The Language of The Goddess,* London, 1989.
— *The Civilization of The Goddess,* London, 1991.
— *The Goddesses and Gods of Old Europe,* London, 1982.
Gover, J.E.B., *Place Names of Wiltshire,* London, 1939.
Graves, Robert, *The White Goddess,* London, 1961.
Green, Miranda, *Celtic Goddesses,* London, 1995.
Grinsell, Leslie V., *Folklore of Prehistoric Sites in Britain,* London, 1976.
Guerber, H.A., *Myths of the Norsemen,* London, 1909.
Guest, Lady Charlotte, *The Mabinogion,* London, 1906.
Gurney, Peter Smith C.S., *Shepherd Lore,* Avebury, 1985.
Hawkes, Jacquetta, *Dawn of the Gods,* London, 1968.
Henig, Martin, and King, Anthony, (ed.) *Pagan Gods and Shrines of the Roman Empire,* Oxford, 1986.
Higgins, Godfrey, *The Celtic Druids,* London, 1829.
Hoare, Sir R.C., *The Ancient History of North Wiltshire,* London, 1821.
Hole, Christina, *A Dictionary of British Folk Customs,* Oxford, 1995.
Hutton, Ronald, *The Pagan Religions of the Ancient British Isles: Their Nature and Legacy,* Oxford, 1991.
— *The Stations of The Sun: A History of the Ritual Year in Britain,* Oxford, 1996.
Jeffrey, David Lyle, *A Dictionary of Biblical Tradition in English Literature,* Michigan, 1992.
Johnson, Buffie, *Lady of the Beasts: The Goddess and Her Sacred Animals,* Vermont, 1994.
Jordan, Katherine, *The Folklore of Ancient Wiltshire,* Trowbridge, 1990.
Keiller, Alexander and Piggott, Stuart, *The West Kennet Avenue, Avebury, Excavations 1934–5,* p. 4. Reprinted from *Antiquity,* vol. 10, 1936.
King, John, *The Celtic Druids' Year: Seasonal Cycles of the Ancient Celts,* London, 1994.
Klapp, W.H., *Murray's Manual of Mythology,* New York, 1935.
Lambeth, M., *A Golden Dolly: The Art, Mystery and History of Corn Dollies,* London, 1969.
Leach, Maria, (ed.) *Funk and Wagnalls Standard Dictionary of Folklore, Mythology, and Legend,* New York, 1984.
Leadbeater, C.W., *Freemasonry and its Ancient Mystic Rites,* New York, 1998 reprint.
Long, W., *Abury Illustrated,* Devizes, 1858.
MacCulloch, J.A., *The Religion of the Ancient Celts,* (Edinburgh 1911) London, 1991 reprint.
— *The Celtic and Scandinavian Religions,* London, 1993.
MacNeill, Máire, *The Festival of Lughnasa,* London, 1962.

Major, Albany F. and Burrow, Edward J., *The Mystery of Wansdyke*, London, 1926.

Malone, Caroline, *Avebury*, English Heritage, 1989.

Matthews, John, *Robin Hood: Green Lord of the Wildwood*, Glastonbury, 1993.

— *Taliesin: Shamanism and the Bardic Mysteries in Britain and Ireland*, London, 1991.

— *The Druid Source Book*, London, 1996.

Meaden, Terence, *Stonehenge: The Secret of the Solstice*, London, 1997.

Mellaart, James, *Earliest Civilizations of the Near East*, London, 1965.

Michell, John, *Megalithomania*, London, 1982.

— *The View Over Atlantis*, London, 1973.

Millson, Cecilia, *Tales of Old Wiltshire*, Newbury, 1995.

Morgan, Morien, *The Mabin of the Mabinogion*, (1901) Northamptonshire, 1984 edition.

Muir, Frank and Jamie, *A Treasury of Christmas: Stories and Pastimes of the Christmas Festival*, London, 1991.

Newall, Venetia, (ed.) *The Witch Figure*, London, 1973.

Nicholls, Ross, *The Book of Druidry*, London, 1990.

Piggott, Stuart, *The West Kennet Long Barrow Excavations, 1955–6*, London, 1962.

Rhys, John, *Celtic Britain*, London, 1904.

Roberts, Jack, *The Sheela-na-Gigs of Britain and Ireland*, Ireland, 1994.

Ross, Anne, *Pagan Celtic Britain*, London, 1992.

— *The Divine Hag of the Pagan Celts*, in Newall, *op. cit.*

Rutherford, Ward, *Celtic Mythology*, Northamptonshire, 1987.

Sjöö, Monica and Mor, Barbara, *The Great Cosmic Mother*, San Francisco, 1987.

Smith A.C., *A Guide to the British and Roman Antiquities of the North Wiltshire Downs*, Devizes, 1885.

Smith, I.F., *Windmill Hill and Avebury: A Short Account of the Excavations 1925–39*, London, 1959.

Spence, Lewis, *The Magic Arts in Celtic Britain*, London, (1945) London, 1996 edition.

— *The Mysteries of Britain*, California, 1993 reprint.

Straffon, Cheryl, *The Earth Goddess: Celtic and Pagan Legacy of the Landscape*, London, 1997.

Streep, Peg, *Sanctuaries of the Goddess*, London, 1994.

Stukeley, William, *Abury Described*, London, 1743.

— *Itinerarium Curiosum*, vol I, London, 1724.

Taylor, F. Sherwood, *The Alchemists*, London, 1953.

Timperley, H.W., *The Vale of Pewsey*, London, 1954.

Trevelyan, Marie, *Arthurian Legends*, (1895) Bristol, 1998 reprint.

Ucko, Peter J., *Avebury Reconsidered: From the 1660s to the 1990s*, London, 1991.

Vatcher, Faith and Lance, *The Avebury Monuments*, London, 1976.

Watts, Kenneth, *The Marlborough Downs*, Wiltshire, 1993.

Williams, Gwyn A., *Excalibur: The Search for Arthur*, New York, 1994.

Wiltshire, Kathleen, *Wiltshire Folklore*, Salisbury, 1975.

— *Ghosts and Legends of the Wiltshire Countryside*, Salisbury, 1973.

Whittle, A.W.R., *Sacred Mound, Holy Rings: Silbury Hill and the West Kennet Palisade Enclosures*, 1997.

Whitlock, Ralph, *In Search of Lost Gods: A Guide to British Folklore*, Oxford, 1979.

— *The Folklore of Wiltshire*, London, 1976.

Wright, A.R. and Jones, T.E., *British Calendar Customs, England*, 3 vols., London, 1936–40.

Index

Aborigines 1
Adam 24, 32, 33, 36
Adam's Grave long barrow 8, 19, 21-4, 32, 45, 47
Afaggdu 61, 101
All Cannings 7, 8, 17, 32
Alton Barnes/Priors 1, 7, 20, 32, 47, 49
Alton Goddess 9, 16, 19–23, 29, 31, 32, 37–8, 40–1, 51, 81, 100, 102, 104
Ann/Anna 16–17
Annwyn 29, 96, 99–104; hounds of 99, 100
Apollo 85–8, 90, 91, 94, 102
Aubrey, John 4, 33–4
Avebury 2, 3, 22, 32–6, 42, 74, 77, 79-95, 97–105; Cove 33, 82

Baubo 71
Beckhampton Avenue 34–5, 82
Beckhampton Cove 35
Befana 67–8
Beltane 49–51
Berchte 67
Berecynthia 40
Black Barrow 19
Bran the Blessed 53, 96–8, 100–4
Bride/Brigit 16, 47–9, 91
bull 13, 64–7
Burl, Aubrey 16, 22, 23, 77

Câd Goddeu 96–7, 100–104
Cailleach 63–6, 72–3, 80, 81
Cain 89
Callanish stone circles 15
Candlemas 49
Cauldron of Inspiration 61, 62, 91, 99
cave art 11, 13, 45

Ceridwen 61, 91, 99, 101, 102, 104–5
Cneph 28, 82
corn dolly 40, 42, 65
Cunnington, M.E. 24–5, 29
cup and ring markings 83

Dagdha 47, 76, 99
Dames, Michael 6, 38, 55, 80, 85
Delos 85, 87
Delphi 85, 87, 102
Devil 77
Devil's Chair 97–9
Devil's Trackway 25, 77
Dodona 85
dove 90, 100
Druids 43, 49, 80, 86, 87, 90, 94, 95, 103

East Field 9, 26, 32, 40
Epiphany 67–8
Eve 24, 32, 33, 35–6

fairies 39, 49
first fruits 39, 85
Freemasonry 30, 90, 91–2

Gimbutas, Marija 14, 21, 55, 60
Glastonbury 8, 48
Golden ball game 49–51
Golden Ball Hill 9, 29, 32, 50–1
Graves, Robert 16, 24, 91, 96, 97, 99, 100, 101, 102
Green Knight 53, 95
Green Man 52–3, 68
Grimes Graves 13–14, 81

Guinevere 9, 96
Guisers 43, 45
Gwion 61–2, 89
Gwydion 96–7

Hallowe'en 44, 45
hawthorn 51, 52
Hogmanay 66
holy wells 16, 48
horse 8, 43–5, 97
Hyperboreans 85–6, 87

Imbolc (see Óimelc)
Isis 29, 70, 90

Jack-in-the-Green 51–3
Jehovah 89
Jesus 67, 91, 92
John the Baptist 53, 77, 90
Joseph 68

Keiller, Alexander 82, 83
Kennet, river 4, 15, 56, 75, 82
King Arthur 8, 60–1, 95, 99, 100–4
King George 46
King Sil 4, 85
King's Throne 97–8, 99, 102
Knap Hill Neolithic enclosure 9, 24–6, 28–32
Koran, the 94, 100

Lady of the Lake 96
lapwing 100, 104
Lugh 42
Lughnasadh 14, 17, 42, 104

Magi 67, 68

Marlborough 53, 96
Martinmas 44
Martinsell Hill 44, 45, 50, 51
Matthews, John 61, 101
May Day 51–3
May King 51, 52
maypole 51, 82
May Queen 51
Merlin 96
Michell, John 82, 93
Milk Hill 8, 9, 19, 38, 47
mistletoe 4, 80
moon 12, 13, 37, 38, 80, 104–5
Morrigán 62, 76, 104
Moses 89, 90, 91
Mummers 44, 45–7

Neck, crying the 39, 40
Neith 85, 90, 91
Nerthus 41
New Grange 45, 99
Nod Cyvrin 87–94, 104

Obelisk, the 33, 82
Óimelc 47–9, 82
omphalos 86–7
Otherworld, the 22, 29, 47, 66, 95, 96, 99, 100–1
ouroboros 81, 83, 84
Overton Hill 34, 79
owl 72, 73

Palm Sunday 44, 50, 60
Paps of Anu 17
Pan 75–7
phallus 14, 79
Pope Joan 69
pyramids 93–4

Pythagoras 87, 94

Ridgeway, the 8, 20, 38
Ringstone 42
Robin Hood 53, 88
roebuck 100, 104
Runestone 94, 104

Saint Anne 16, 17, 42
Saint Bride/Brigit 16, 47, 49
Saint Catherine 82
Saint Patrick 73
Samhain 43–4, 65
Sanctuary, the 34, 35, 79, 82
Santa Claus 67
Senchan 62
serpents 24, 26–7, 28, 32, 33, 34, 36,
    47, 71, 82–5, 87
Sheela-na-Gigs 68–73, 90
sickle 65, 73
Silbury Hag 57–60, 63, 65, 73, 74, 76,
    81, 96, 99
Silbury Hill 3–6, 15, 21, 38, 56, 57, 60,
    63, 64–5, 73, 75, 77–8, 80, 81,
    84–7, 96, 99, 104–5
Sir Galahad 99
Sir Gawain 53, 61, 95, 104
Stonehenge 2, 8, 37, 86
Stukeley, William 4, 34–5, 81–2, 84,
    92–4
Sutton Benger Green Man 52
Swallowhead spring 15, 56, 60, 74, 75,
    99

Taliesin 61, 89, 90, 91, 99, 101, 102
Tan Hill 8, 16–18, 38, 42, 43, 81, 104,
    105
Tan Hill Fair 8, 17, 42, 43
Thor 62
three degrees 91–2, 93
triangular enclosure 9, 29, 38
triangular stones 29, 30

umbilical cord 9, 24, 26, 27, 29, 32, 40

Vale of Pewsey 1, 2, 7, 9, 15, 37, 38, 54,
    95, 104, 105
Virgin Mary 16, 68, 90

Waden Hill 59
Walker's Hill 8, 19–20, 23, 38
Wansdyke 23, 99, 100, 101, 102
Washer-at-the-Ford 62, 63
water meadows 57–59
West Kennet Avenue 22, 33, 34, 81–4
West Kennet long barrow 3, 21, 22, 75,
    79–80, 81, 99
Windmill Hill 22, 31, 79
Winterbourne 57, 58, 64, 73, 74, 75, 81
Winterbourne Monkton 73
Woden 23–4, 97, 100, 103
World Tree 85, 97

yoni 28, 29, 90

Zeus 85, 87